PAPERCUT
LANDSCAPES

Sarah King

SEARCH PRESS

Dedication

To Matt, Amy and Hannah, Sylvia and Ed, with thanks for your love, encouragement, humour, patience and support of my creative pursuits!

Acknowledgements

Thank you Ann Martin of *All Things Paper* who featured my work in her blog (allthingspaper.net), which led to this opportunity; to Katie, Edward, Paul and the team at Search Press for making this first book journey smooth, memorable and enjoyable. Thank you also to Emma King, of *Bluebirds and Paper*, and Lisa Daniels, of *The Flittermouse*, for allowing me to use their work on pages of this book. Finally, thank you to my lovely friends, customers and followers for your enthusiasm, constructive criticism, feedback and banter.

First published in 2019
Search Press Limited
Wellwood, North Farm Road,
Tunbridge Wells, Kent TN2 3DR

Illustrations and text copyright © Sarah King 2019

Photographs by Paul Bricknelll at Search Press Photographic Studio

Photographs and design copyright © Search Press Ltd. 2019

ISBN: 978-1-78221-566-0

Publisher's note
All the step-by-step photographs in this book feature the author, Sarah King, demonstrating her papercutting techniques. No models have been used.

You are invited to the author's website:
appleseedpapercuts.co.uk

CONTENTS

INTRODUCTION

I first discovered papercutting about four years ago, when I was looking for an affordable way to make art for our home. Inspirational quotes were appearing everywhere, so I sat at the kitchen table with a thick black pen, a craft knife (which I had no idea was blunt) and some photocopying paper, surrounded by four blank walls waiting to be filled with framed words of wisdom.

From this less than auspicious start, and despite having no formal art training, I found my naïve drawing skills translated really well into papercuts. I discovered a new hobby that would take me to the unexpected status of papercut artist! I'm writing this book to help you discover and share my enjoyment of this peaceful, creative and colourful pastime.

Some cultures have been cutting paper for thousands of years, for decorative, ceremonial and practical purposes. It's popular today because you need very few inexpensive tools to create beautiful gifts and artwork, often using just one sheet of paper which you can then enhance with colour or embellish in many different ways.

You can draw your own pictures, download templates online or find them in books like this. The techniques are easy to learn – just add patience and confidence for a good result!

I'm going to show you how to take the single-sheet, silhouette-style papercut to a different level by adding colour. I've learned some tricks to make the process easier and quicker which I'll share in this book. You'll find some smaller projects to practise your skills, and a range of coast and countryside-inspired landscapes of varying difficulty to cut and colour with paper.

I really hope you will enjoy creating your papercut landscapes as much as I do and that this book will inspire you to craft your own, colourful art – with just a knife, paper and time.

Good luck!

Opposite:
A selection of seafaring papercuts, inspired by sunny days at the beach.

MATERIALS

Papercutting is a brilliant craft for beginners as you can practise with the most basic of materials – you need only a pencil, eraser, craft knife or scalpel, a piece of paper and a cutting surface.

   Anything you don't already have at home can be bought online or in craft shops. In the UK you must be eighteen years or over to buy knives and blades. Check the rules of the state or country that you are in.

   Once you have a general idea of the skills and techniques needed, you will naturally be drawn to experiment with different knives and types of paper, different cutting surfaces and even different glue and applicators.

KNIVES

Your cutting tool will be comprised of a handle and a blade. They are inexpensive to buy and last many years. You will find some handles more comfortable than others and you will also develop a preference for certain types of blade. Over time, you will find a favourite knife to work with.

   Knives come with lids – use them! These razor sharp tools should be respected – never leave your knife unguarded on a table top or desk. Mine has its lid on and is put in a zipped pencil case in a drawer at the end of every cutting session.

   The three types of knife commonly used for papercutting are:

STATIC BLADES

Most papercutters work with craft knives and scalpels that have a replaceable blade locked in a fixed position. Held like a pencil, a static blade requires you to use more of your arm and to turn your paper as you work (especially when you are learning).

Scalpels are incredibly sharp surgical instruments which usually have a metal handle that can be flat or round. I find round handles more comfortable to use because you can gradually roll them between your thumb and forefinger as you cut curves. Popular scalpels for paper craft are: Swann-Morton number 1 round handle or a number 3 flat handle; paired with 10, 10a, 11 or 15a blades. Fiskar's soft-grip art knife is also a comfortable choice, and it can be used with different brands of blade.

Craft knives tend to be cheaper to buy than scalpels and will still create sharp, clean cuts. They have slightly thicker blades, which can be an advantage – even if you're heavy-handed, you are unlikely to snap a craft knife blade. Popular makes include Xacto and Jakar which come with their own brand of blades. Craft knife blades are typically more expensive than scalpel blades, so make sure you shop around.

SWIVEL KNIFE

Held like a pencil, a swivel knife consists of a barrel-shaped handle with replaceable blades. The blades are much shorter and less flexible than scalpel blades, which means they work well with thicker paper and card. Unlike knives with static blades, the blade in most swivel knives is set in a plastic pivot which allows it to rotate 360° while cutting. This makes it good for cutting circles and curves. Although some people find swivel blades have too much movement, I now use a swivel knife for every aspect of my papercuts, including long, straight lines!

FINGERTIP KNIFE

To use a fingertip knife, you slide your index finger into the looped handle, then hold it as though it is a pencil, driving it with your thumb and middle finger. It is easily controlled for both fine detail and cutting long edges. A useful knife, the blades are sturdier than scalpel blades, and come in fixed or swivel variety.

SPARE BLADES AND STORAGE

When you buy your first knife, buy extra blades and expect to change them often. To give you an idea of how many you will need, a typical papercut in this book is approximately A4 – that is, 210 x 297mm (8¼ x 11¾in) – in size, and will require between ten and twenty blades, depending on the detail it contains, the paper you use, your cutting surface, and how hard you press. Some people like to change the blade regularly – after every fifteen minutes of cutting is a common approach – but after a while you will know when the blade needs changing by the quality and 'feel' of the cut (see page 17). Using a blunt blade is a risk which can have disastrous effects on your beautiful piece of work! Blades often cost less the more you buy, so consider buying in bulk.

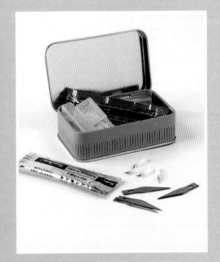

It goes without saying that you should keep your new and used blades in a safe place, away from children and animals. How you dispose of blunt blades will vary depending on where you live. In some areas, the local authority, pharmacy or doctors' surgery will handle the disposal of used scalpel blades if you collect them in a special sharps box that can be purchased online. This is the safest method, but is dependent on the service being available to you. As an alternative, speak to your local refuse and recycling services to find out what they recommend. Until disposal, store any used blades in a lidded tin or jar, out of harm's way.

PAPERS AND CARD

One of the most common questions from new papercutters is 'What paper should I use?' When choosing papers, your first consideration is the weight. Most of the world measures in grams per square metre (gsm), but some territories, notably the USA, measure paper weight in pounds per ream (lb). Because the two systems are not directly related, the numbers do not necessarily correspond. As a general rule, however, the heavier the weight, the thicker the paper.

Photocopying paper – the kind you can buy in supermarkets for your home printer – is usually around 80gsm (20lb). It is not good enough quality to make great papercut art but is fine to practise using your knife on.

Most papercutters prefer weights between 90 and 160gsm (around 108lb). Origami papers can be much lighter, around 60gsm, and can give very interesting effects; but I prefer to use card – which can be anything from 160gsm up – for my landscapes because it gives more depth to my designs and is thick enough to be glued securely without wrinkling. The paper you use really is a very individual choice and the only way to find what you like is to try as many types as you can.

Believe it or not, the back of the paper you choose for your silhouette cut – the outline cut that all your smaller infilling blocks will be stuck to – is also important. Why? Because your design will be drawn/printed onto the reverse of your sheet. You'll cut it out and then turn it over to the 'good side', where your cuts will look neater and any drawn/printed lines will be hidden.

So it helps if the back of your good paper (i.e. that which will end up in the finished piece) is a light enough colour for you to see your drawing/printed lines. Paper which is white on the back and coloured on the front is known as 'one-sided' or 'single-sided'. This is a good option if you want your papercut outlines to be darker colours (instead of the white I favour). You can also buy 'poster' paper which is black on the front and light grey on the back.

The thickness of paper/card you choose will depend on the project you're working on and, crucially, how comfortable you find it to cut. Lightweight papers can tear very easily, while heavier papers/card can make your hand ache. Newsprint, light card, book pages, magazines, even wallpaper and wrapping paper can all be experimented on with varying degrees of success. You will find your comfort zone over time.

A4 or US Letter paper is the best size to use for the templates in this book. If you are going on a papery shopping spree, here are some common papers to try:

- **Textured card** This can give you interesting effects. DoCrafts Papermania offer a capsule box of seventy-five coloured, textured 216gsm sheets.

- **Hammered paper** Lightly textured, as though flattened all over with a tiny hammer, hammered paper comes in different thicknesses, with 160gsm being popular for cutting both the outline and the coloured infills. You will find around fifty different colours and this paper is favoured by many papercutters.

- **Coated paper** Some papers have a white 'core' which means they have been coated with a colour, rather than dyed all the way through the sheet. When you cut coloured paper with a white core, you may see the white fibrous edges in your cuts. Make sure your blade is always sharp to avoid this, or choose paper/card with a coloured core.

TIP

If you are drawing your own designs, use lightweight white paper for your sketch. This will allow you to turn it over and hold it up to the light to reveal how it will look from the right side after it has been cut. This is very useful when drawing things backwards! Just photocopy, scan and print, or use tracedown paper to transfer your finished drawing onto the back of your good paper.

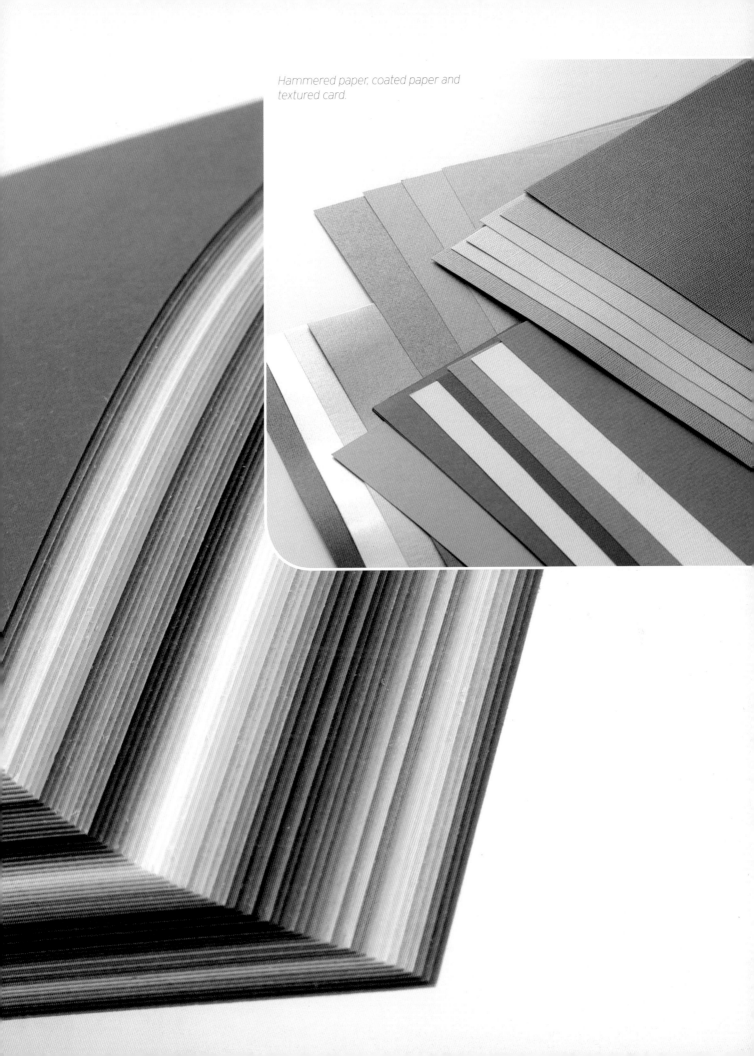

Hammered paper, coated paper and textured card.

OTHER MATERIALS

Pencil and eraser I love mechanical pencils with an eraser at the top for sketching my designs, but any pencil and good quality eraser will do.

Cutting mat There are two main types of cutting mat available – self-healing or glass. They come in a range of sizes, with A3 – 297 x 420mm (11¾ x 16½in) – suiting most papercutting needs. A self-healing mat provides a comfortable, plastic-coated cutting surface, which allows the blade to pass through the paper. The mat then closes up, leaving no trace of the cut in it. Most come with grid measurements of both centimetres and inches, and are available in all standard paper sizes. If you look after your cutting mat by following the care instructions – washing occasionally in warm soapy water and using different parts of the mat to cut on – it can last the hobby papercutter six months or more. If you can see or feel nicks in the surface, then turn it over or replace the mat, as scratches can draw your blade in unwanted directions while you cut.

You can buy glass cutting mats specifically for crafting but a smooth kitchen worktop saver made from tempered glass is just as good. Glass lasts much longer, is easy to clean and is good for very fine work, as the paper cannot sink into the mat while being cut. However, there is less resistance on the blade, which can make it feel slippery.

Glue Your glue should be acid-free so it does not discolour your paper over time. Sometimes you will be applying glue to areas just millimetres wide, so a glue pen such as the Sakura Quickie Glue Pen, which has a fine nib for pinpoint accuracy, is ideal. The glue goes on blue and dries clear. It is also repositionable for a short time.

Pritt Stick/Power Pritt is good for paper as it does not cause wrinkling. If you are sticking tiny areas, use a cocktail stick or even a blunt scalpel blade to take tiny scrapes of glue and apply carefully in spots. Never drag the glue stick over the back of your papercut (to add a piece of backing card, for example) as you are likely to tear the paper or dislodge some of your carefully placed coloured infills.

PVA glue is great for papercuts made from card or paper over 160gsm/220lb in weight. Use very thin spreads rather than dots on lighter paper to avoid wrinkles.

Glue spreader or applicator You will need a tiny glue spreading device. Some paper artists use a cocktail stick to spread tiny smears of glue from a stick. Others use a blunt scalpel blade. For PVA, a fine paintbrush can be used (wash it after, or it will set solid), or even a cotton bud (cotton swab). You can buy refillable glue applicator bottles which are also often used for paper quilling. My personal favourite is a colour shaper. This is a tiny rubber-tipped tool for sculpting clay (stolen from my partner's man-cave!), which is perfect for spreading PVA or solid glue on small areas.

Tracedown paper, tracing paper or a photocopier/scanner The quickest way to copy your design onto your good paper is with a photocopier or scanner. If you do not have access to these, tracedown paper or tracing paper can be easily used (see page 24). Tracedown paper comes in black (for tracing onto light papers) or white (for tracing onto dark papers).

Masking tape A useful tape to have to hand; this allows you to keep paper in place on your cutting mat if cutting through more than one sheet at a time; to make minor repairs; or to secure coloured layers on the reverse of your papercut, as an extra measure.

Metal ruler Useful for measuring, and also if you need to cut straight lines with your knife. It is important that it is metal – otherwise you will chop chunks out of your nice wooden or plastic ruler (or worse, your fingers).

White pencil Occasionally you may need to sketch your design onto paper or card which is black or very dark on both sides. A normal pencil won't show up very well on black, so a soft, white pencil, or even a chalk pencil, is handy to have.

Fineliner pen You may decide to go over your pencil sketches with a fine pen, so the lines are clearer for cutting. Rub out the pencil afterwards for clean copying of your design.

Guillotine Access to a guillotine is not essential, but it is really useful to create true, straight edges on your finished pictures, to get them ready for framing.

Lamp Having a directional lamp that you can aim straight onto your work will help to prevent eye strain. Wireless lamps are available if your cutting area is not near a plug. Lamps with a daylight bulb/setting will enable you to see truer colours.

Top row to bottom row, left to right:

Mechanical pencils and eraser; cutting mats; glue sticks; glue applicator and colour shaper; tracedown paper and tracing paper; masking tape; metal ruler; white pencil; fineliner pen; guillotine and portable dayight lamp.

GETTING COMFORTABLE

Now we have our materials, let's get comfortable. Papercutting can be very mobile. You can work at a desk, on the kitchen table, out in the garden, or in front of the television with a lap-tray on the sofa. But it is also completely absorbing, and without noticing, it's easy to find you've been sitting in the same position for hours. So make sure you are sitting correctly and take plenty of breaks to move around, to avoid neck, back, head and shoulder aches.

TIPS FOR COMFORT

- The work surface should be high enough so that you don't have to bend over it and deep enough so that you can rest your forearms on it while you work. If you get uncomfortable quickly, make adjustments to the height of your work surface or to the chair, or put your feet on a low stool under your desk. (I raised my desk onto blocks of wood to make it a comfortable height, for example.) You could also try using a sloped writing board on your desk.
- Unless you're in good daylight, you will need to set up your lamp so that the shadow falls behind your cutting hand and not across the area you are trying to cut.
- Remove any watches or bracelets that could snag or dent your paper as you cut. I also like to roll up my sleeves. Tie long hair back so it doesn't get cut by mistake – it does happen!
- Sitting down for long periods of time is bad for your health. If, like me, you're prone to working without realizing the time, listen to radio shows, short audio books or an album – when it's finished, get up, walk around a bit, stretch your arms and neck, make a drink, then carry on.

TECHNIQUES

The following basic techniques will give you some practice in using knives in various ways, and build up to cutting out a silhouette papercut – after that, you'll be ready to look at colour and tackle the projects.

USING A KNIFE FREESTYLE

First we are going to practise using a knife. We'll use a fixed blade scalpel, a swivel knife and a finger knife in turn to make some test cuts on a piece of paper. If this is the first time you have used a knife, I recommend you try some freestyle cutting – that is, without following any lines – on a sheet of copy paper before you head straight into a template.

Your aim when cutting freestyle is to feel comfortable and to get used to handling and holding the knife. Once you can make freehand cuts on your everyday paper, draw some straight lines, circles, zigzags, squares and wavy lines and have a go at following them. Be bold – make sweeping freehand cuts, straight and wavy lines, zig-zags, circles, squares. Keep it simple and larger to begin with and don't worry about accuracy or tidiness.

I often hear the phrase 'hold the knife like you would a pen'. However, this doesn't take into account that people hold their pens in different ways and some people find they change their grip when using a knife. The key points are that the cutting edge of the blade needs to be at around forty-five degrees to your paper, and the blade needs to be perpendicular to the paper; not tilted.

To prevent tears and slips, keep the paper taut by using the index finger of your non-cutting hand to hold down the paper while you cut away from it.

STATIC-BLADED KNIFE FREESTYLE

Hold your scalpel at a forty-five degree angle to your paper. I'm using a scalpel for this technique: a Swann-Morton Number 1 handle with a size 11 blade, in fact. However, the details of the static-bladed knife you use are largely irrelevant. Instead, choose one that feels comfortable while you work.

How to hold a static-bladed knife for freestyle work.

1 Draw a line using an HB pencil, then put your index finger near the far end, to hold the paper or card. Holding the scalpel as shown above, begin to draw it slowly along the line using pressure similar to that needed to write with a ballpoint pen.

2 Keeping the angle of the knife to the paper the same, draw the scalpel down a little way. When you reach a curve, turn your wrist to keep the cutting angle constant and the blade perpendicular.

3 Move your finger down a little to keep the paper secure, then continue to the end of the line.

SWIVEL KNIFE FREESTYLE

Unlike the scalpel, you don't need to adjust the angle of your wrist when using a swivel knife. The blade itself will swivel to help you cut curves.

1 As with the scalpel, hold it as described opposite. After drawing your line, hold the paper in place with your finger, then begin to draw the blade down the line, working away from your finger.

2 Simply use the swivel knife like a pen, as though drawing the line.

3 Continue to the end of the line. As with a static-bladed knife, don't go too far in one go. Stop moving the blade, move your finger down to just behind the knife, then carry on.

FINGERTIP KNIFE FREESTYLE

When attaching the blade to a finger knife, make sure that it is the right way up, with the handle the right way. Finger knives can be found with either fixed or swivel-type blades.

1 Slip your index finger through the handle, supporting it with your middle finger and thumb.

2 The fingertip knife is otherwise used like a scalpel; follow the instructions above to practise.

WHEN TO CHANGE YOUR BLADES

A blunt blade will 'gather' the paper along with it and cause it to tear in fragile places. It can also stretch the paper, create fluffy edges, or have a dragging feel while cutting. If your hand starts to ache, it could be because your blade is blunt and you are having to press harder. Change your blade as soon as you notice any of these.

It's not worth carrying on with a blunt blade with the thought that 'it'll do'. A blunt blade can lead to you ripping your papercut – or even slipping and cutting yourself. You could also end up having to neaten some already delicate areas of work, which increases the risk of cutting away so much that you lose the original shape.

CUTTING STRAIGHT LINES

As a new papercutter, you will probably be most comfortable cutting your straight lines from north to south; towards you. With practice, however, you will move the knife in directions you didn't think were possible!

If you are cutting a long, straight line, position the paper so that you can complete the cut in one movement. If you feel like you are running out of room (or cutting mat!), stop, lift the knife and move the paper along, then reinsert the knife where you left off and continue.

Turn the paper round if necessary so that the line on your template is positioned at an angle comfortable for your hand to travel smoothly in one direction.

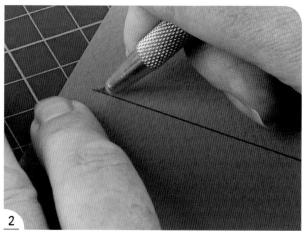

1 For longer lines, position the paper at a similar angle to that shown. As you move your arm in one smooth movement, you will naturally work slightly towards the same side of your body as that which you are cutting.

2 Place your blade at the far end of the line, holding the paper with your hand.

3 Draw the blade in one smooth, controlled movement. Keep your wrist straight and move your whole arm.

4 Aim to complete the line in one go. Confidence is key to getting a long straight line.

Shorter straight lines

For short lines, you can keep the paper closer to you, and work at less of an angle. This will give you more control.

CUTTING CORNERS

For the neatest corners, cut from the centre of the corner outwards. Cut the first
line, lift out the knife, return to the centre of the corner and cut the second line.
You may need to turn your paper around when you do this.

1 Set the paper up at a comfortable angle so the first
line is facing you, and put the blade on the corner itself.

2 Cut down the line as for a straight line (see opposite).

3 Put the knife down safely, and turn the paper so the
other line is facing you.

4 Place the blade in the corner again.

5 Draw down the second line to finish the corner cut.

CUTTING GENTLE WAVES

Wherever possible, gentle, wavy lines should be cut in one movement so that they are smooth. You may find you have to move your hand and wrist more with a fixed blade than with a swivel blade. If you are running out of room or your hand is at an awkward angle, stop mid-way, lift the knife out, move the paper along then reinsert the knife where you left off.

1 Set up the paper as for a straight line, with the gentle waves at a slight diagonal, and cut down the line, working from the far end and using the knife like a pen.

2 As soon as the movement starts to feel awkward or uncomfortable, put your knife down and move the paper away from you, keeping the angle constant.

3 Starting from the point where you lifted off, reinsert the knife and carry on cutting, following the line like a pen.

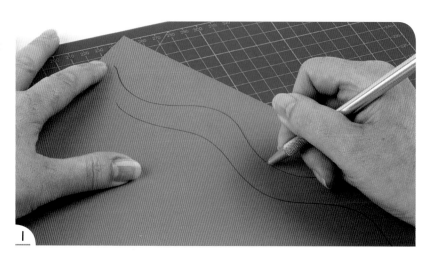

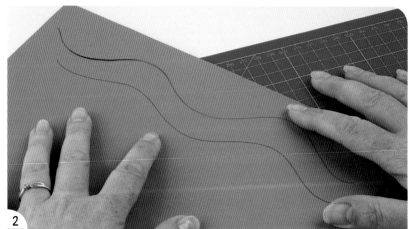

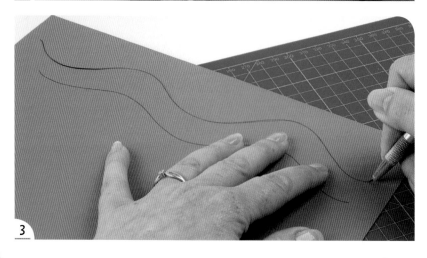

CUTTING CHANGING SHAPES

Shapes that change from thick to thin – like a crescent or a teardrop shape – can be tricky to cut. Start with the widest part, where the paper will be stronger, and cut to the thinnest part. If you cut from the thinnest part to the thickest, you could tear the paper. The idea behind this technique is to put the tension of the knife's 'drag' on the strong, widest part, rather than on the weak, fine point.

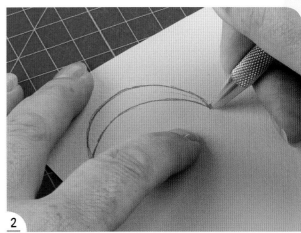

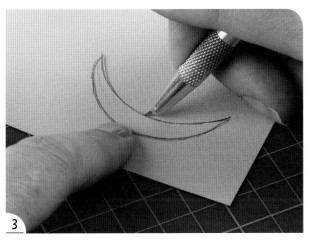

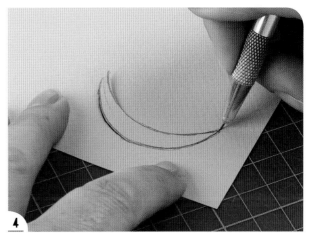

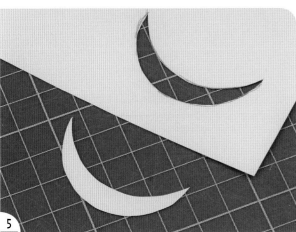

1 Cut one end at a time. To start, insert the blade at the centre of the longest side, at the widest part of the crescent.

2 Draw the knife down the curve, stopping at the point of the shape.

3 Lift the knife out and reinsert the blade at the widest part of the shorter side. Turn the paper if you need to.

4 Draw it down to the same point. One point is now cut.

5 Repeat the process to cut the other end of the crescent. Remove the shape.

CUTTING LARGE CIRCLES

If you're using a fixed blade, you may prefer to turn the paper, rather than the knife, as you cut your circle. Try experimenting with cutting in both anticlockwise and clockwise directions, as people often have a preference. You could also make lots of short, straight cuts to start with, which will get curvier as you practise more – with some practice you will also be able to gently rotate a round-handled knife as you cut.

   As a guideline for using a fixed blade or a swivel blade, you can cut about one quarter of the way around a circle the diameter of a coffee mug before you need to pause to turn the paper before carrying on.

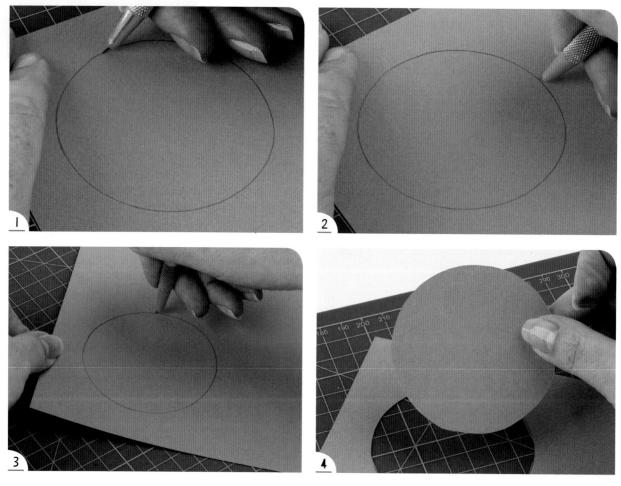

1 For large circles, start at the top and draw the knife roughly a quarter of the way round, until it starts to feel uncomfortable, at which point stop.

2 Keeping the point in, hold the knife upright, and rotate the paper beneath the blade until the point becomes the top of the circle.

3 Cut the next quarter of the circle, then repeat.

4 Carefully lift the circle out.

CUTTING SMALL CIRCLES

As the circles get smaller, you will find that a swivel knife requires less paper turning, but a static blade may require more. If you are cutting tiny circles with either fixed or swivel blades, make lots of short cuts – sometimes just stabs – and keep turning the paper. Eventually you will find the smallest circles you can cut to be around 2mm (1/16in) across.

TIP »»»

For really, really tiny circles, forget the knife and invest in a pokey tool! This is like a thick needle used to poke tiny holes. To keep it neat, poke through from the right side of the papercut to the back.

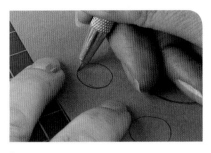

1 For small circles, a swivel knife is a real asset - it will allow you to cut further and more smoothly round the circle.

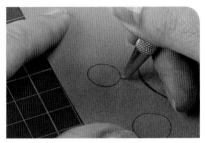

2 Here I have been able to cut halfway round or more in a single movement.

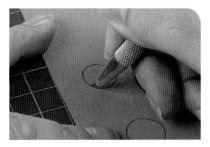

3 If the circles are small enough, there is no need to move the paper; just start from the top again and cut round the other side.

23

REMOVING CUT-OUT PIECES

Some papercutters leave all the cut pieces in the papercut until the end as it can help to keep the integrity of the paper intact. However, I'm too impatient and like to see progress as I'm cutting intricate pieces, so I lift mine out as I go!

To remove a piece, just dab it with your knife blade and it should lift out cleanly – if not, recut the area and try again. Don't pull out a stuck piece – you'll end up tearing the paper and leaving tufts of fibres.

TRACING

To create a colour-filled papercut, you will need two copies of your template. One will be on your good cutting paper. The other will be on everyday copy paper and will be used to cut through to create your coloured shapes. The easiest way to do this is to use a scanner or photocopier to reproduce the templates from the book. Alternatively, you can use tracedown paper or tracing paper, if you prefer.

USING TRACEDOWN PAPER

1 Place your good paper face down on the table – you want the template to be transferred to the back, not the right side.

2 Lay a sheet of tracedown paper over the top. If you are using a dark paper, use white tracedown paper to help make the finish clear. Tracedown paper doesn't have a facing, so it can be either side up.

3 Place the template face-up on top of the pile.

4 Using an HB pencil, start to draw over the white lines of the template. Fill in the lines completely, rather than making a single fine mark – this will ensure you have a good thick line to cut, which makes things easier later, and makes the silhouette nice and sturdy.

5 Continue to fill in the lines, making sure that you fill in the whole design.

6 As you work, peel back the template and tracedown paper to check that the image is transferring correctly.

7 Be sure to transfer the border of the design too, to make sure that the whole design is included.

8 Remove the template and tracedown paper to reveal the transferred design. You can re-use both, so don't throw them away.

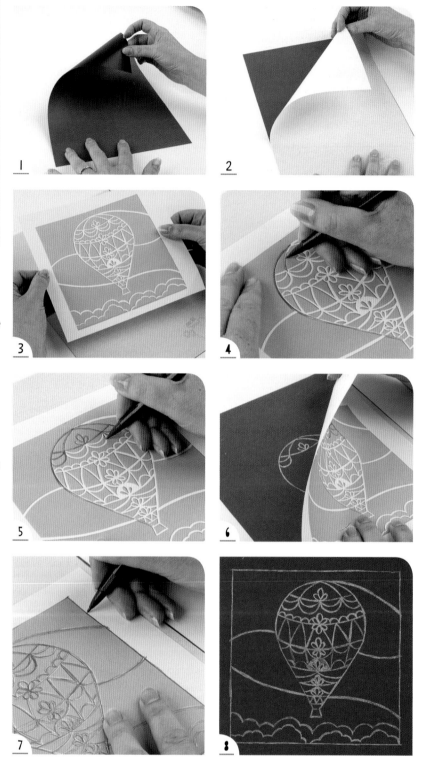

24

USING TRACING PAPER

1 Lay the tracing paper over the design.

2 Use a soft pencil, such as a 4B, to carefully trace over all of the lines. Fill them in, rather than making very fine lines. This takes a little more time, but will make your cutting much easier later.

3 Be sure to include the borders.

4 Turn the tracing paper over, and place it face down on a piece of scrap paper to protect the surface. Still using the 4B pencil, work over the lines once more from the back.

5 Turn the tracing paper over once more, so that it matches the design, then lay it on the back of your good paper. Still using the 4B pencil, scribble firmly over all the lines to transfer the image.

6 Lift away the tracing paper to reveal the design (see inset).

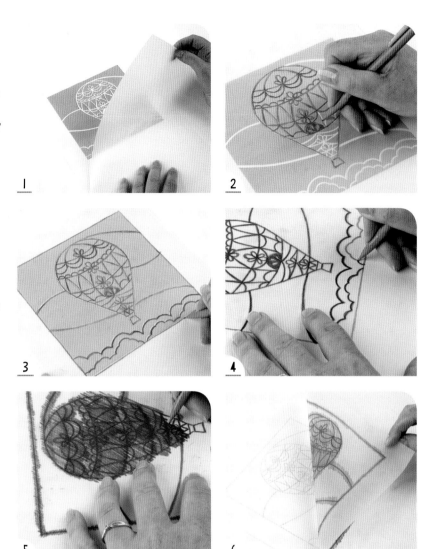

ANOTHER APPROACH

If you do not have tracedown paper or tracing paper, you can simply put your design on top of your good paper and secure both pieces to your cutting mat with masking tape. You can then cut through the design and your good paper underneath. Carefully remove the masking tape and the top template sheet and you will be left with your papercut at the bottom.

CUTTING THE SILHOUETTE

A finished silhouette cut.

Now that we've practised cutting straight and curvy lines and circles, it's time to try a picture. One of the most common questions from new papercutters is 'Which bits do I cut out?' In this book, you will cut away all the coloured spaces from the templates, leaving the white lines of the drawing intact. The result is a 'silhouette cut', to which we can add colour at a later stage.

For this exercise, you will need to perform several different manoeuvres with your knife – sweeping lines, points, and semicircles. Don't forget: you are cutting away the grey areas. Use the index finger of your non-cutting hand to hold the paper down, then cut away from that finger. This will help reinforce and steady the paper.

When cutting, we always cut from the back so that the cuts are sharp when viewed from the front. Once you have finished cutting, you'll be turning over the cut; and so any pencil lines will be hidden on the reverse. The finished cut will face the opposite direction to the template; a mirror-image.

THE SILHOUETTE PAPERCUT

Here are the four basic stages of a silhouette papercut:

1 **Copying** Copy or draw your template onto the back of your nice cutting paper.

2 **Difficult cutting** Start cutting out the parts you think will be the trickiest - if you make a mistake, you can begin again without having got too far.

3 **Simpler cutting** Continue cutting from the middle of the picture working outwards, and from closed to open areas. Leave any big pieces until the end so that the paper retains its strength throughout the cutting process. Change your blade regularly.

4 **Tidying** Once you have cut the entire image, put a new blade in your knife and tidy up any edges or corners.

The template for this exercise, provided at actual size.

STAGE 1: COPYING

1 Copy the template (see pages 24-25 for techniques for copying) once onto copy paper, and once onto your good paper. Put the copy to one side – this will be used for the colour, later.

STAGE 2: DIFFICULT CUTTING

We start with the more challenging areas to cut simply because if we make a mistake, we can start again with the least wasted effort.

2 Place the good copy on your cutting mat and begin to cut out the shapes. Start with the most difficult parts of the design – in this case, the decorations in the middle of the balloon.

3 Continue cutting away the patterns on the inside of the balloon. Feel free to turn the template to help with your cutting.

TIP »»

Pick the paper up occasionally and turn it over – this is a quick way to check whether you have missed any sections, or to see if any edges need tidying.

STAGE 2: SIMPLER CUTTING

In general, try to leave the largest sections of grey in place as long as possible, as these help to retain the integrity of the paper, and will help to support the rest of the cut.

4 With the difficult section completed, move on to cutting out the simpler parts: beginning with the middle sections of the sky.

5 Cut out the top section of the sky. You can cut the borders freehand, as long lines (see page 18), but if you prefer, use a metal ruler to help guide you. Be sure to hold it very firmly and keep the blade as close as possible to the ruler. You may want to practise on scrap paper first.

6 Cut out the bottom section of sky, then the tops of the trees. Cut the upper section of treetops first, then move on to the ones nearer the bottom border.

STAGE 4: TIDYING

7 Check the finished template and tidy any areas that need work. If you've worked carefully and used a sharp blade, you shouldn't have too much to tidy.

7

The completed silhouette cut.

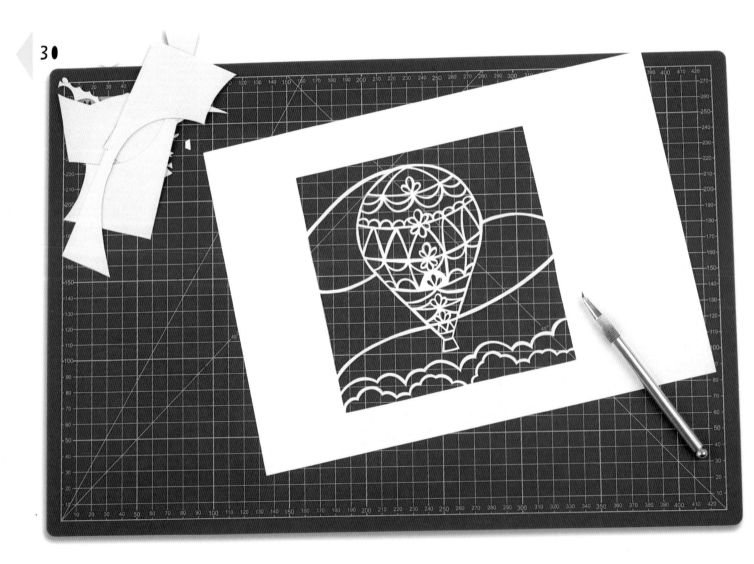

TROUBLESHOOTING

How did you get on?

OOPS, I CUT A BIT OFF BY MISTAKE!

If the missing piece doesn't affect the overall picture, just carry on regardless. If it's a major piece of the image, you may have to start again. But you could first try to fix the odd piece back together as shown:

TIP »»»

You can also repair small mistakes with a dab of PVA glue across the join on the back – just make sure it's dry before you carry on cutting, and don't stick it to your mat by mistake!

1 Identify the mistake from the front.

2 Turn the template over and use a sliver of masking tape to repair the slip, trimming away any overlap with your knife.

3 Turn the template back over and check the repair is invisible.

WHY ARE THERE LOTS OF FLUFFY BITS?

If the fibrous core of your paper is showing as fluffy bits along the edge of a cut, which often happens in corners or on long edges, you could find a permanent pen that matches the paper colour and dab it gently on the back, so the ink stains the white fibres.

Alternatively, use a sharper blade to recut the area more cleanly, as shown here. Resist pulling out pieces of paper that aren't cleanly cut at the corners because this will leave fibres – go back and carefully recut the part so it lifts out freely.

Recut the area more cleanly to remove fluffy bits.

If a fluffy area appears in a corner, cut from the inside point outwards.

MY PAPER LOOKS LIKE IT HAS STRETCHED

A blunt blade can stretch paper and card – just change your blade regularly to avoid this happening. Sometimes you can smooth down a stretched part once you add the infills, but it doesn't always work. You can either start again or carefully trim out the stretched piece if the design can work without it.

THE EDGES OF THE PAPER ARE RAISED

Occasionally, when you turn your papercut over, the cut edges are slightly raised. This is usually due to the paper being pushed down very slightly into the self-healing mat as you cut with the knife. It is easily solved by rubbing the back of your fingernail against the edges to smooth them down.

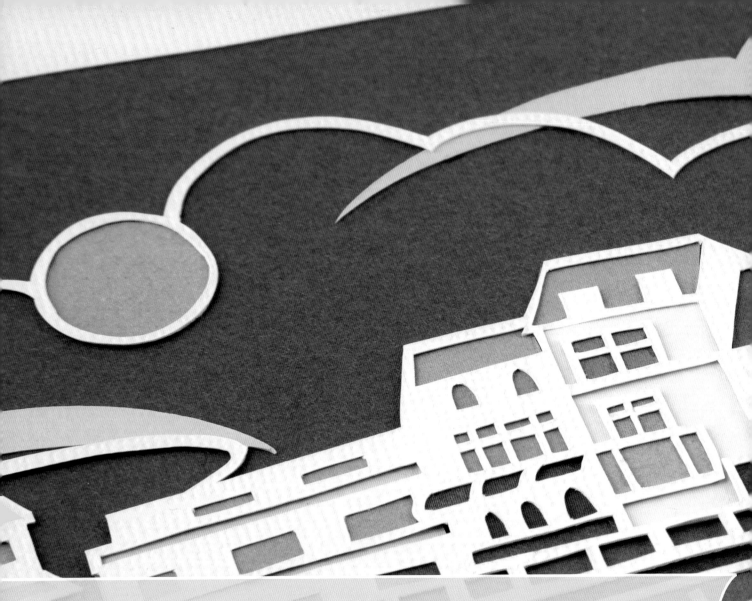

ADDING COLOUR

When you first start adding colour to your work, you will become over-excited about your amazing new skills, and rightly so. You'll add colours to everything, convinced that the viewer will be so impressed with your technical ability with a knife that they will fall in love with your art on the spot.

But here's the thing. Choosing the right colours for landscapes is as important as being able to cut and fix them! If your colours don't match or contrast well and the feeling of the piece becomes confused or flat, your technical ability may as well not exist.

Papercuts executed with precision knife-work can be let down by poor or confusing colour choice, and will end up discarded in drawers. I've restarted landscapes myself after stepping back and realizing that the colours aren't giving the effect I was after.

Adding colours to a landscape gives layers of feeling to your work – you're creating a piece of art that should be pleasing to the eye and evoke a mood in the viewer, be that happiness, peace or even loneliness or menace. Your colours should be chosen carefully to reflect this.

In short, your colours need planning.

Bold colours reflect the heat of the sun in this harbour-side papercut.

CHOOSING COLOURS

I prefer to choose my colour palette before I start cutting any infills. I usually choose between ten and twenty colours for a detailed landscape. These are the things to consider:

MOOD

Before you start choosing your colours, decide on the overall mood you wish to convey. The season and weather are good places to start. You may look at a template in this book and decide there's a storm brewing, or perhaps it's night-time. Maybe there's snow on the ground. Is the sea choppy or calm, or is it a warm, hazy day? All these things will affect your colour choice.

POSITIONING

Sometimes you will have a collection of things together such as trees or rooftops of similar colour. Try not to put the same colours next to each other, otherwise one of two things will occur – your neighbouring objects will lose their definition and become lost, or they will become a large group of one colour which dominates the landscape.

TEXTURE

Some papers are textured on one or both sides, so you need to decide which side of the paper you want visible in your finished cut – which side is the 'right side'.

TINY DETAIL

Tiny details, such as distant house windows, need strong colours to show through a papercut outline, especially if you use card (over 160gsm/220lb) for your silhouette cuts.

LARGE DETAIL

The sky, sea or fields can seem like the easiest infills to do. However, for large expanses, you may need to break the space into two or three shades or different colours to stop it looking flat and lifeless.

CONTRAST

You also need to avoid colouring objects the same as their background colour. For example, a yellow beach hut on a yellow sandy beach will get lost, or your hot air balloon will look like it has holes in if you colour its patterns the same blue as the sky. Choose different shades or different colours.

BALANCE

Look for one or two colours that you can reflect from one part of the landscape into another so that the picture feels structured. For example, you can take one shade of blue from the sea and use it again in part of the sky. Or a green from the grass at the bottom of the image could be picked out again in the leaves of the trees near the top.

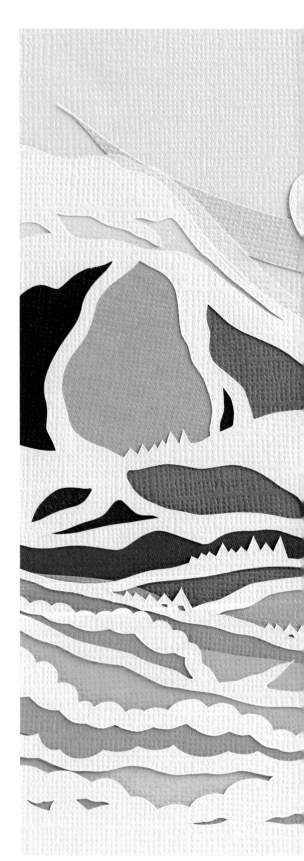

Contrasting palettes

The mountain views above and on the next page have been created from the same template, but changing the colours has created two strikingly different moods.

MAKING A DECISION

Once you have picked the colours you want to use, take a few moments to double-check before you begin. Place all your chosen colours side by side – do they match and contrast well? Are there any that don't fit? You don't have to understand the technical reasons why colours work or don't work – trust your instinct and change anything that jars the eye or doesn't feel right.

If you are struggling to imagine what colours you need, try colouring in a copy of the template first (see below) then matching the coloured copy to your papers. If you're using software to create your own template designs, you can also experiment by filling the colours in on your screen then choosing paper to match.

Colour plan

Colouring the picture gave me an idea of which colours to place where and showed me what would and wouldn't work. Once I finished the example above, I realized the mountains had lost definition at the bottom. To fix this in the finished piece, I replaced the green and purple pencil colours with shades of grey paper.

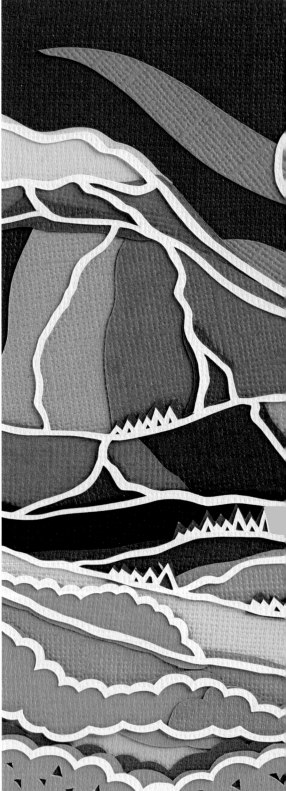

COLOURED INFILLS WHERE TO START?

A good rule of thumb is to infill the objects in front of other things first, then work backwards. There are three main reasons I work like this:

• To create the correct order of depth;
• To give my infilled papercut strength;
• To save time.

With more complicated landscapes, keeping infills in the right order can take a bit of working out, but the principle remains the same.

Take a look at the hot air balloon you cut earlier (see page 30). The hot air balloon is in front of the sky. The lowest layer of trees are in the foreground. The second row of trees is further back and the sky is behind everything else. You could colourfill the trees first, or the hot air balloon. I'd start with the hot air balloon because it's the most interesting part of the cut and, frankly, I can't wait to see what it will look like!

INFILLS AND TOPFILLS

· **Infills** are glued to the back of the silhouette cut.

· **Topfills** are added to the front (the right side of the papercut).

The template for this exercise, provided at actual size.

38

HOW TO CUT INFILLS

Have to hand the following:

- A copy of the original template on copy paper: either a printed copy or a tracing of the template from the book.
- Your knife and spare blades.
- A spare, clean gluing surface next to your cutting mat (I am using an old cutting mat here).
- Glue suited to the paper/card you are using: a glue pen, PVA glue and small spreader, or glue stick.
- A sheet of white or neutral coloured card big enough to cover the entire landscape – this will be glued over the reverse at the end to tidy up the back and secure the infills.

1 First, place your silhouette papercut with the right side down on your clean gluing surface.

2 Decide which is the right side of the coloured paper you are using, then put it right side down on your clean cutting mat. Place the template copy on top of the piece of coloured paper and hold it in place. Use your knife to cut round the shape that you want to fill (marked A¹ opposite) cutting through both the copy paper and the coloured paper. Cut along the centre of the white outlines. This ensures the coloured piece you cut is large enough to fill the shape, while remaining small enough not to overlap the edges.

3 Discard the top shape, then remove the coloured shape.

4 On the silhouette papercut, use a glue pen to carefully apply glue to the edges where the infill will go.

5 Use the point of your knife to gently dab and lift the cut-out piece onto the glued area of the silhouette cut.

6 Press it down with your finger to secure.

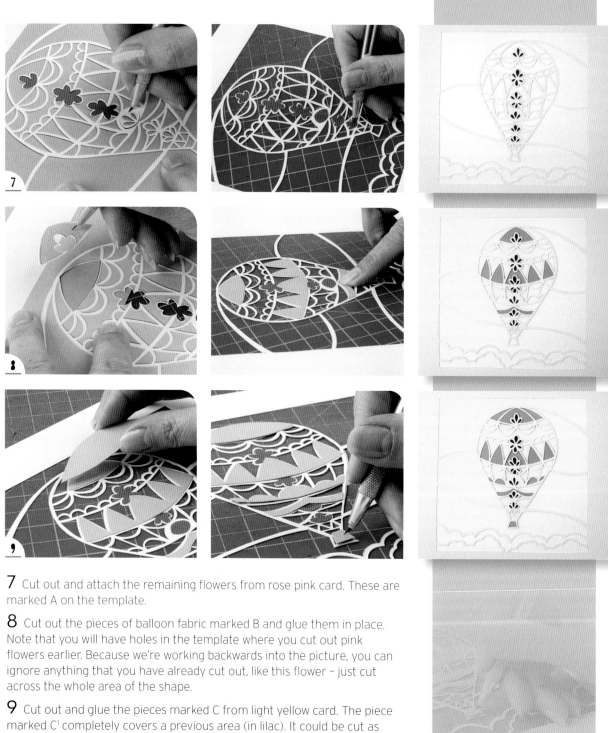

7 Cut out and attach the remaining flowers from rose pink card. These are marked A on the template.

8 Cut out the pieces of balloon fabric marked B and glue them in place. Note that you will have holes in the template where you cut out pink flowers earlier. Because we're working backwards into the picture, you can ignore anything that you have already cut out, like this flower – just cut across the whole area of the shape.

9 Cut out and glue the pieces marked C from light yellow card. The piece marked C¹ completely covers a previous area (in lilac). It could be cut as two separate parts to place on either side of the lilac section, but using one large piece to cover the whole area makes your piece sturdier – and it's much faster, too.

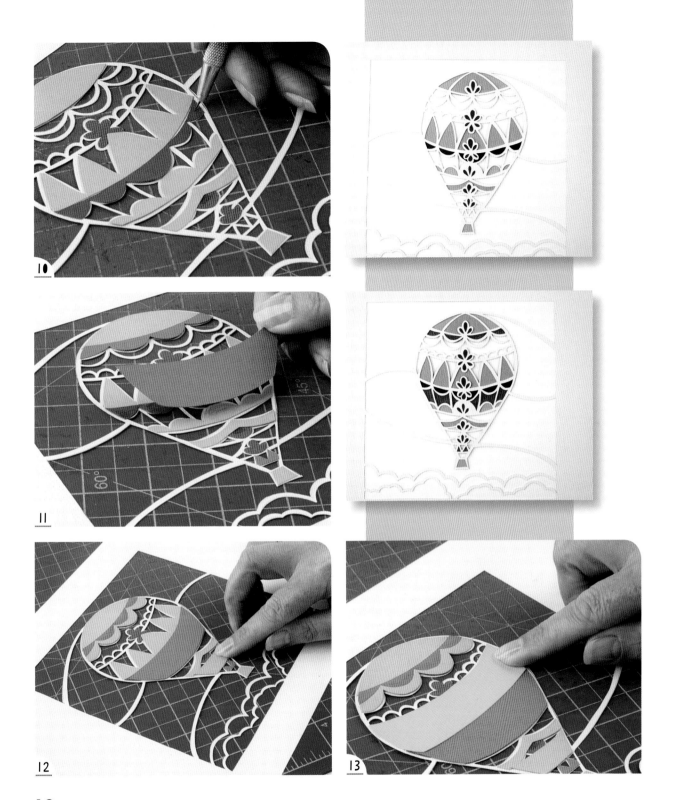

10 Cut out and glue the parts marked D on the template from purple card. Again, you can cut single large parts to cover these areas.

11 Do the same for the pieces marked E on the template, using coral card.

12 Use mid yellow for the parts marked F.

13 Use light green for the parts marked G.

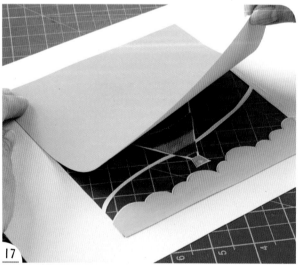

14 Use purple again for the parts marked H.

15 Change to dark green for the parts marked I, which includes the foreground trees as well as the final part of the balloon.

16 Adding the background trees (J) with light green completes the main image. Once all your colours are fixed, make extra sure that all the pieces are secure and that the reverse looks tidy.

17 To finish, cut a single large panel of light blue to cover the back of the whole piece. This will help support and protect the smaller, more fragile pieces. Secure this with PVA or glue stick, rather than the glue pen - such a large piece requires a stronger bond.

Using the practice piece

If you want to turn this piece into a finished papercut to display, glue a piece of white card across the back of the entire picture (see inset). You can also trim all the edges with a guillotine or scissors to ensure the picture is central. Now you have finished your first papercut with coloured infills! What do you think?

HALF-HOUR TEMPLATES

Many papercutters tell me they are scared to add coloured infills because they don't want to risk ruining their beautiful silhouette papercut. So here are two templates specifically for you to practise with, which will take no more than half an hour to cut out, and give you lots of scope to practise some of the skills covered further in this book. Experiment with fewer – or more – colours of your choice. You could even change the sun in the first example into the moon!

SUNRISE

This first piece features a sunrise – or, with the right choice of colours, a sunset – over fields. As in the exercise on pages 38–43, colourfill the objects in front of other things first – the bushes (in front of the fields) and the sun (in front of the sky). Then work from the bottom upwards. This will give you the advantage of cutting your striped field infills slightly deeper so that they can overlap each other on the back, giving a sturdy gluing platform.

Infills that extend to the edges of the picture can also be cut wider than the template edges so that they will overlap onto the frame around your silhouette papercut, again giving you extra secure gluing space.

44

> **TIP »»»**
>
> A glue pen is ideal for the fine lines of the outlines, but larger areas benefit from some additional strength in the form of PVA glue. Use a thin glue spreader to apply PVA to the shape, then place the piece on top.

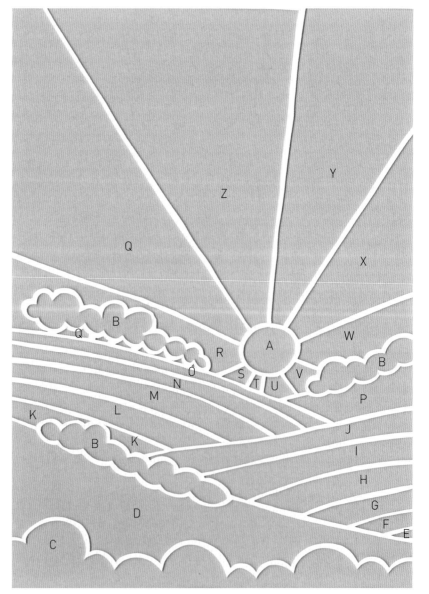

The template for this exercise, provided at actual size.

LIGHTHOUSE

For the lighthouse cut, colour the bushes in the front first (A), then the path (B) and the grassy bank (C). Then colour the cliff face (D) followed by the sea (E). Fill the base of the boat (F) and the star on the sail (G) then add the sails and the flag (H and I). Fill the door (J and K) and windows (L); then the rest of the lighthouse (M and N); and the bushes behind the lighthouse (O). Fill the sun (P) and finally the sky (Q).

The template for this exercise, provided at actual size.

PAPERCUTTING THE LANDSCAPE

The following pages of projects highlight different techniques and ideas to focus upon. At the start of each, I have provided some hints and tips along with a suggested order of work, but my hope is that you'll add your own little touches and ideas to these designs in order to make them your own. Change the mood, use more or fewer colours, or add topfills.

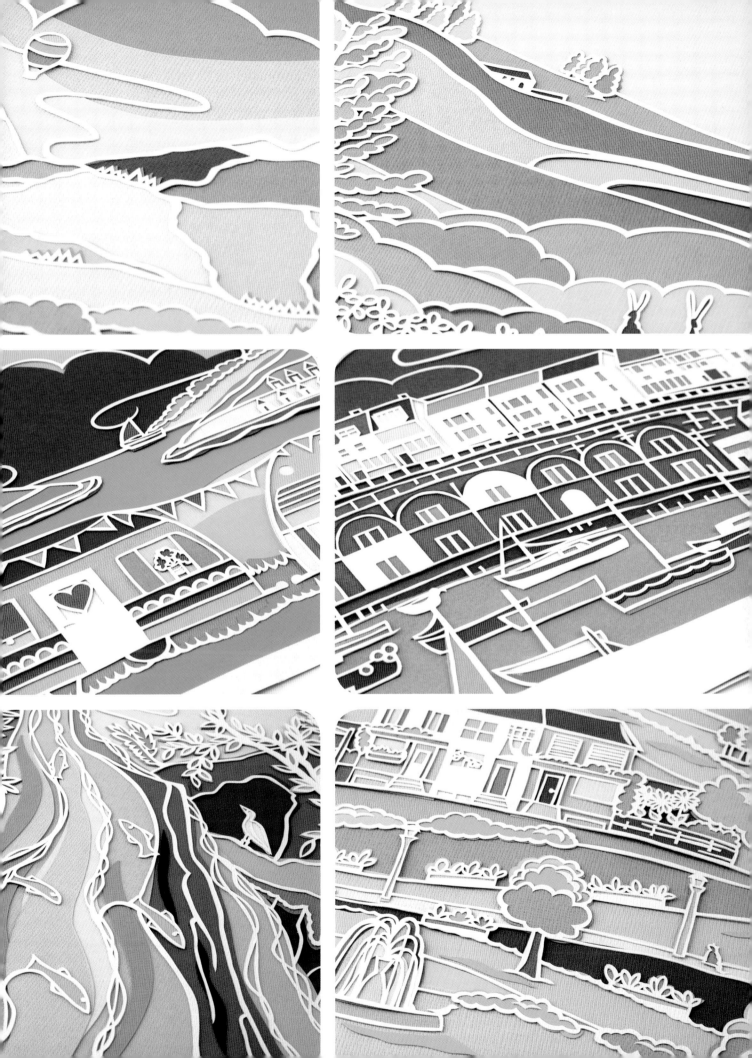

Basking Balloons

I went on a hot air balloon trip with my mum once. It was an amazing experience, so I am very fond of them and often put balloons in my pictures to add colourful detail to summery skies.

When you are designing your own papercut, remember that any objects in the sky need to be connected to an anchoring line so they don't just fall off the page when you cut them out. In this picture I used one wavy line, to represent a gentle breeze that passes through each of the balloons and connects at opposite edges of the picture.

50

YOU WILL NEED

Papers: one A4 (US Letter) sheet of copy paper; one A4 (US Letter) sheet of 160gsm white paper or card; one A4 (US Letter) sheet of 160–220gsm card; selection of 160gsm paper or card in different colours

Knife: cutting knife and spare blades of choice

Glue: glue pen, glue stick and PVA glue with spreader

Other: metal ruler

PROJECT HINTS AND TIPS

When choosing your colours, bear in mind that it's best not to use the same colours on the balloons as those you use in the background. Otherwise, your balloon will appear to be invisible. I used a small amount of blue in the rainbow-coloured balloon and made sure it was darker than any of the blues I chose for the sky.

I used 160gsm hammered paper to colour this picture and a combination of glue pen for tiny edges and PVA glue. I like PVA because it's quick and easy to spread, and very secure. However, when gluing large pieces, like the hills and sky, or the treetops across the bottom of the picture, be very careful not to use too much PVA. 160gsm paper is quite thick to cut but will wrinkle or bow very quickly with excess glue.

If your piece does start to bow, putting a heavy book on it straight away should flatten it out. If your infill paper is lighter than 160gsm, or you're worried about gluey drips ruining your carefully cut out silhouette cut, use a cocktail stick, or even a blunt scalpel blade, to scrape glue from a glue stick and smear dabs on the paper instead.

ORDER OF WORK

Start by colouring the balloons first because they are in front of the sky and the hills, and the trickiest parts of the cut. For the background scenery, work from the bottom row of trees and progress up the page as it goes into the distance.

When you have completed all your coloured infills, apply a fresh piece of paper or card across the entire reverse of the picture. I use a glue stick for this part as it provides a secure hold and will be wrinkle-free. This will secure your infills and neaten up the back of the piece.

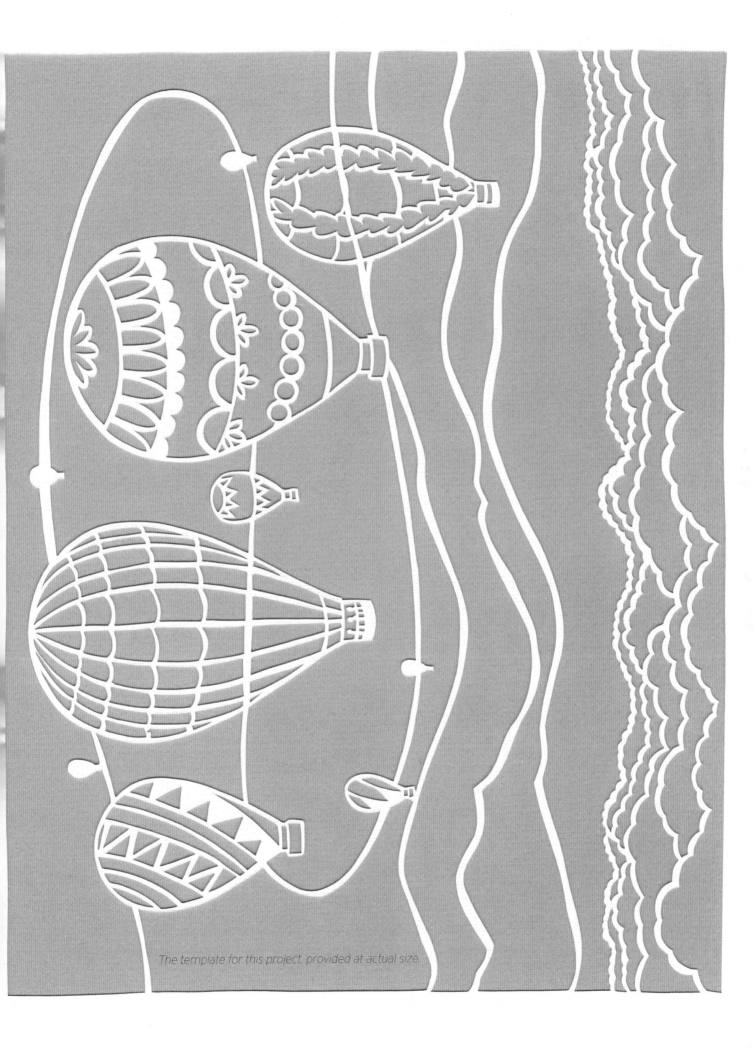

The template for this project, provided at actual size.

Focus on... Building layers of colour within objects

1 Following the steps for the exercise on pages 38-43, fill in the tiny details of each balloon in turn first.

2 Use the glue pen for fine edges.

3 Use a combination of a glue pen for the fine edges, then a dab of PVA glue or glue stick on parts that are already infilled, for extra security.

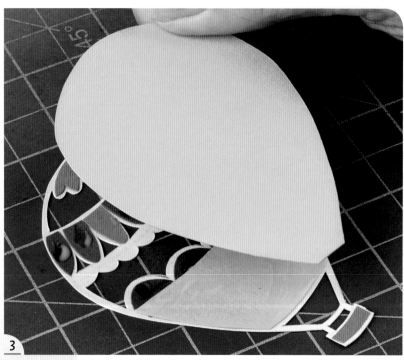

The finished example.

Focus on... Freehand sky

In this cut, you will notice that the coloured paper in the sky doesn't follow any of the template lines. That's because I decided to cut two lighter blue infills freehand to give more movement to the sky. To do this, use what is left of your template to identify the width and depth of the paper infill you need, then cut one wavy line or sweeping line across the width of your coloured paper. When you have cut your two pieces, turn your sky infills right side up then hover your papercut right side up over the infills, to see how they look. Have a play around with the positioning of the pieces – sometimes I intend an infill to be at the bottom of the sky but decide to turn it upside down and put it at the top instead! When you're happy, glue the lighter blue pieces in place, then cut one large rectangle of darker blue that will completely cover the space between the two lighter blue pieces and glue it down.

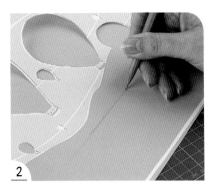

53

TIP ›››

In this case, the width is almost exactly right, so there's no need to make a mark for that here. However, if you have a small sky area to fill, or a large piece of sky background paper, mark the width as well.

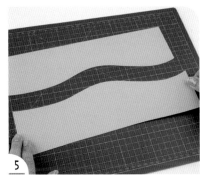

1 Use what is left of your template to check the width and depth of paper you need to fill the sky area.

2 Leaving a little extra at the edges, use an HB pencil to mark the bottom of the area you need (see also tip above).

3 Put the template to one side, then cut the sky background paper roughly to size.

4 Cut a freehand wavy line across the whole width of the sky background paper.

5 Turn the sky background pieces over, so they are right side up, and move them apart slightly.

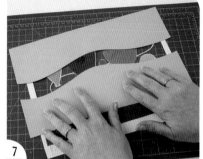
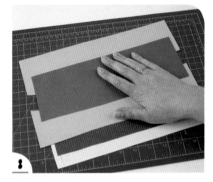

6 Next, hold the papercut right side up over both pieces to check how it will look. (Note that the papercut here is simplified, for clarity). There should be a gap in the centre of the sky as shown.

7 Glue the two sky pieces in place on the back of the papercut.

8 Using a different blue paper or card for contrast, cut a piece large enough to fill the gap, then stick it in place on top of the other sky pieces.

9 Turn the papercut over to reveal the finished sky then trim any excess to finish.

The finished project

There's no sun in the sky, but the use of warm colours suggests this balloon fiesta is taking place on a hot, dry day. Hot air balloons are perfect for experimenting with bright splashes of colour and patterns.

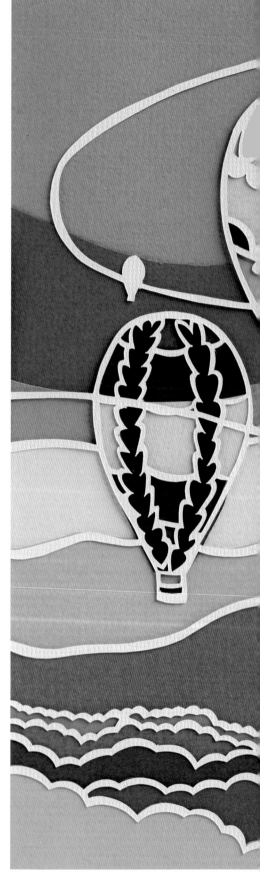

Mountain Scenery

This template has already been seen earlier in the book, on pages 34 and 36, in two different colour schemes – one snowy and one darker. This time I amended the template by drawing a simple hot air balloon in the sky, then added a spring feel with coloured infills.

I thought you would like the chance to try this template too, following one of my colour schemes or using one of your own.

PROJECT HINTS AND TIPS

Think about how many different shades of colour you will need for the fields and the mountains. I recommend at least four different shades or colours for the fields and at least four for the mountains, so that you can space them out.

ORDER OF WORK

Colour the objects in front of others first – the balloon and the bushes/fir trees, then work from the bottom of the scene up to the sky. At the end, fix one piece of card across the reverse of the piece to complete the picture.

YOU WILL NEED

Papers: one A4 (US Letter) sheet of copy paper; one A4 (US Letter) sheet of 160gsm white paper or card; one A4 (US Letter) sheet of 160–220gsm card; selection of 160gsm paper or card in different colours

Knife: cutting knife and spare blades of choice

Glue: glue pen, glue stick and PVA glue with spreader

Other: metal ruler

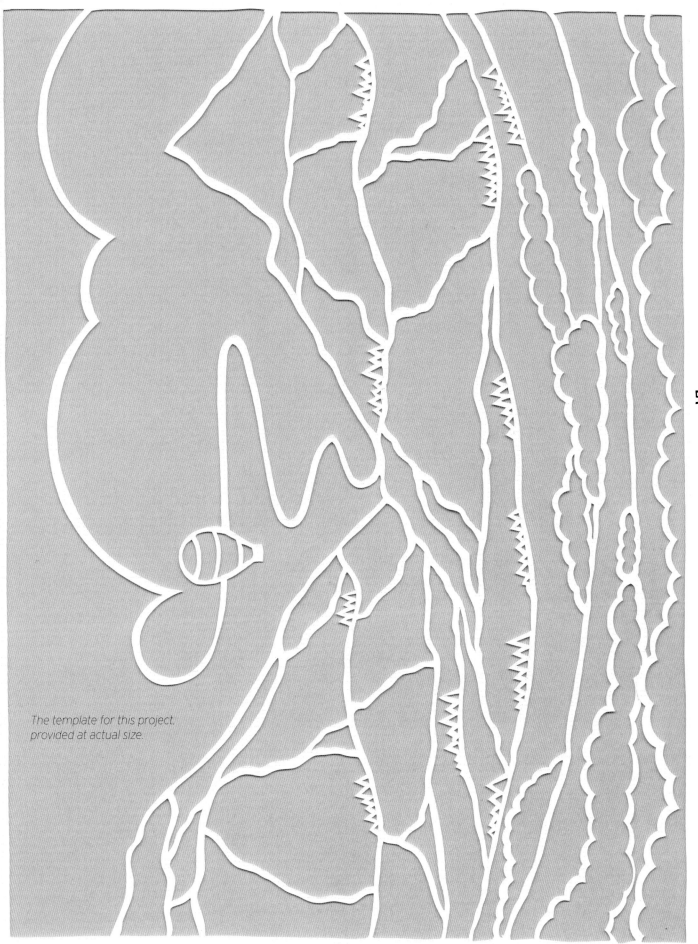

The template for this project, provided at actual size.

Focus on... Cutting oversized infills

Make your infills more secure by cutting those that extend to the edge of the frame slightly wider or longer than the template. For example, the bushes along the bottom edge needn't stop right at the edges of the template. Just freehand extend them by 5mm (¼in) at the sides and along the bottom. Then, when you glue the infill to the back of the silhouette papercut, you will have an extra edge that you can fix to the frame of the cut.

You can apply this thinking to many of the infills in this picture. For example, if you look at my version, you will see an olive green field on the left. This looks like it is precisely cut to fit – all the visible parts are. What you cannot see at the back is that I extended the size of the olive infill by a few millimetres at the side and also a few millimetres along the bottom, so that I had extra olive card that I could glue to the yellow infill to make them both more secure.

Cutting oversized infills isn't necessary but it can be a very useful tactic for making your work sturdier and, sometimes, easier to cut.

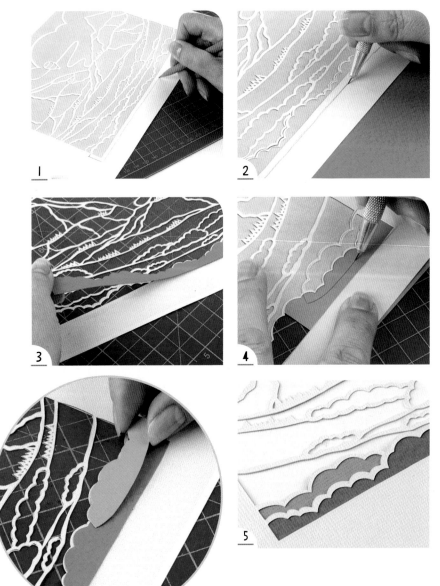

1 I have used a pencil to mark the extra 5mm (¼in) margin for this example, but there's no need for you to do this - it's perfectly fine to simply extend the shape into the frame by eye.

2 Cut the piece out as normal, working beyond the frame at the edges.

3 When you come to glue the piece on, you now have some extra surface at the edges. This not only secures this piece more strongly, but will add to the overall strength of the papercut. Perhaps most importantly, it helps to avoid any gaps in the finished piece.

4 When adding later pieces, you can include an extra margin not just at the edges, but into gaps left in the template from earlier pieces. Here, I am cutting an oversized shape for this small piece of hedge that incorporates part of the margin and part of the foreground hedge.

5 The oversized shape can extend behind the margin or other completed areas as far as you like - though there's no need to waste paper, so a margin of 5mm (¼in) or so is generally sufficient. The result won't be visible from the front.

Focus on... Customizing the design

When adding an element to a design, it must connect to another line of the design, or to the edge. When trying this out for the first time, I suggest making pencil lines as thick as the other lines of the design. With experience, you can use a simple fine line.

1 Use an HB pencil to clearly mark your addition to the template. Here, I'm adding a balloon, which I'm connecting to an existing cloud line.

2 If you want to add something to an empty area of the design, you will need to add a line that connects it to the edge or another part of the design. Try to build this naturally into the design - here I have added a cloud line to connect a new balloon to the edge of the design.

3 When removing elements from the design, use the pencil to clearly cross out any parts you don't want to use - like this balloon. I also need to fill the gap left, so I have drawn a strong line to connect the two parts of the cloud line.

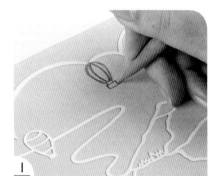
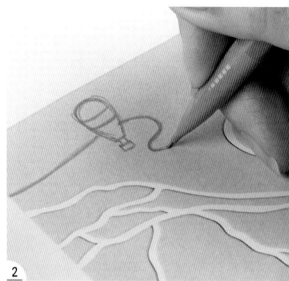
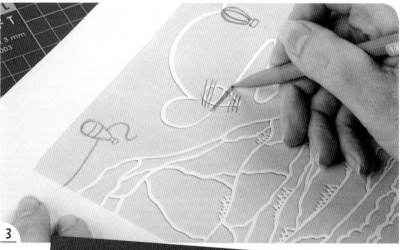

This variation was made using the template on page 57 - note the central balloon has been removed, which, along with the muted colour scheme, lends a less playful feel to the piece.

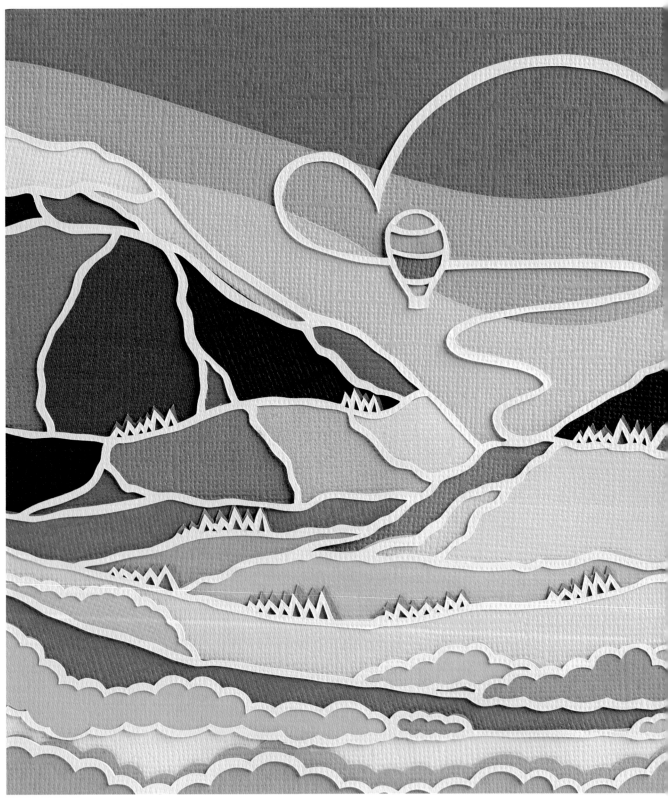

The finished project

There's a slight chill in the air of this picture, created by choosing an icy blue in the sky that meets the snow-covered tops of the mountains. I bet it's nice and warm beneath the burner of the balloon, though!

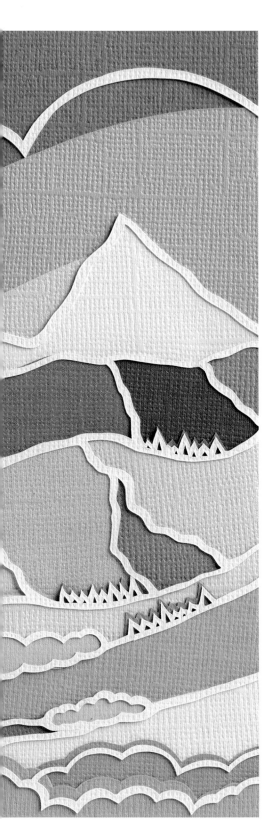

Small is beautiful
Use strong colours in small spaces so they show through.

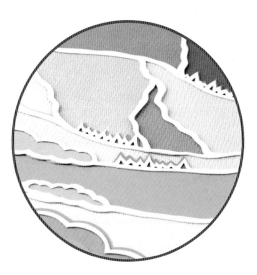

Variety
Varying the shades of the colour in the mountain adds interest.

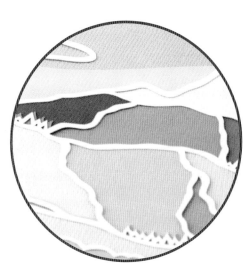

61

Extra details
A colourful hot air balloon adds a playful detail to the scene.

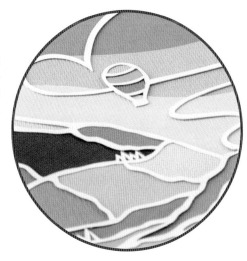

Heath by the Sea

Inspired by the heather-coloured, sea-reaching heaths at Lands End in Cornwall, I designed this template to practise ordering the infills from front to back and to use colour to give depth to the finished artwork. You will also be an expert in cutting small circular/oval shapes by the end!

PROJECT HINTS AND TIPS

The most complicated parts of this image – and the most time-consuming – are the tiny flowers at the front. Even though you are only using the point of the blade for the tiny ovals, it will become blunt, especially if using a glass mat. An early indication of this is having to press harder to make the cuts, at which point change your blade and give your hand a rest if necessary!

There is the possibility that you will make mistakes and chop off petals or even stalks! Don't worry – small mistakes really won't notice here and, if the piece still supports itself, just carry on.

ORDER OF WORK

First study the template and look for objects that are in front of other things as these will be coloured first. You should have spotted the following: the flowers right at the bottom; the hares in front of a grassy bank; the little house on the hillside. Then the trees, all of which are in front of something else. Even the trees on the horizon are in front of the sky, as is the sun. You can colour these pieces in any order, though I prefer to start with the fiddliest bits first to get them out of the way; in this case the colourful heather in the foreground.

Once your tiny details are coloured, we can start placing large pieces of colour behind them without the need to cut around the little pieces again. If you have tried using colour in your papercuts before and found it frustrating trying to piece all the bits together, you will find this process much easier and quicker with practice.

TIP »»»

Should you decide to amend the template, you will also need a pencil and eraser.

This is the order of work I followed, but you don't have to follow it precisely. As long as you work from front to back, you won't go wrong.

The template for this project, provided at actual size.

Focus on... Choosing a colour palette

When choosing your colour palette, think about the season or the weather you wish to convey. Are you going to use muted, moorland tones? The reds and oranges of autumn? Or perhaps it's night-time, with moon-gazing hares. Maybe abstract is more your thing!

If you have trouble choosing colours, try colouring in a copy of the template first, as shown below. Keep all the pencils you use to one side then match them to your paper. You could also number the pieces on the template in the order that you want to fill them, which is helpful if you have groups of similar shapes overlapping one another, like in the grassy foreground of this template.

Focus on... Groups of trees

Groups of trees look unnatural and dull if they are all the same colour. A grouping all in the same colour will also tend to dominate the image. To avoid this, we can build them up gradually. Some trees will be nearer the front than others, so colour the ones at the front of the group first, then the ones behind them.

When you are colouring a group of trees which are clearly defined in the template, you will need to think about two things – the order to fill them and the colours.

1 Identify the frontmost tree; we'll start with this because we can use this as a 'sticking platform' to help support the other pieces that go behind.

2 Cut the shape for the frontmost tree and glue it in place.

3 When adding the subsequent infills, try to vary the colours as much as possible and avoid using the same colours on adjacent spaces. If possible, keep the silhouette cut near to you, so you can quickly check the colours you've already used to help choose the colour for the next area.

4 Cutting oversized infills (see page 58) will help to make the piece sturdier.

5 As well as looking at the pieces as separate areas, try to think of them as complete trees – parts of the tallest tree here, for example, can also be seen at the bottom of the group, so treat them as one big infill.

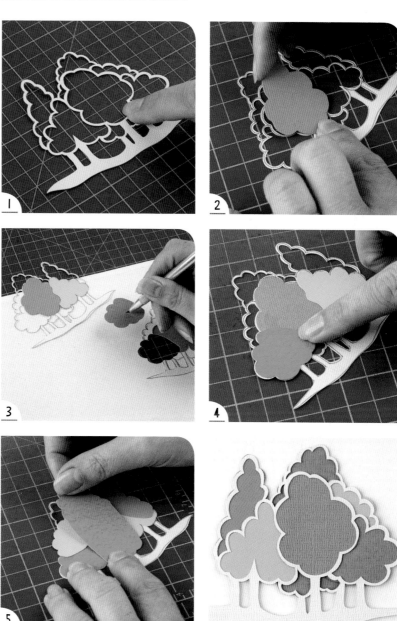

The finished effect.

Focus on... Cutting tiny shapes/ filling flowers

On page 65, we looked at colour-filling individual trees within a group. Here we are going to colour sections of flowers from within a bigger group.

Whilst I cut the flower infills tightly to the template outlines in my finished piece, you could follow the steps below to cut loosely round sections of flowers. This is less time-consuming, easier to manage and will also give the finished piece more movement.

1

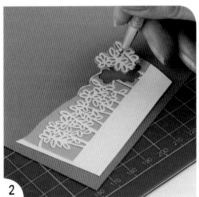

2

3

4

1 For very small areas like these individual flower petals, where there is not enough room to draw the knife, use a series of small stabbing cuts that overlap to release the shape.

2 For areas with lots of very small parts close to one another, doing individual infills would be hugely time-consuming, and not particularly effective - better to use larger group infills. Look for natural groupings. To the right of this piece on the template, for example, there are three flower stems. Cut loosely round the whole group.

3 When gluing the loosely-cut infill in place, don't be obsessed with keeping it within the lines - as long as there are no gaps within the shapes, some overlaps at the edges will add a sense of movement and interest.

4 Continue until the area is filled.

The finished project

The orange, mauve and hot pink make the picture pop and add interest to areas with no other detail in them. To give some balance to the picture, I've reflected the greens from the near fields to the far fields and groups of trees, and the flower colours match the heaths.

Love Blooms

On a visit to the Victorian walled garden at Quex Park in Kent, I was struck by the huge, ornamental poppies in the borders – so they have turned up here as the foreground to this romantic, hillside garden picture.

In this piece, you will get the chance to practise colouring trees, use freehand cutting for the sky and fill a multitude of small shapes in groups.

PROJECT HINTS AND TIPS

If you look closely at the finished picture, you will notice that a lot of my infills extend beyond the outline of the object. This is an effect I like to use to give a sense of movement and fluidity. The flowers appear to be in a gentle breeze or to have a haze around them. I achieve this simply by cutting loosely around the template shape instead of exactly along the lines. Sometimes I cut the infills slightly bigger, other times I undercut the size of the required piece and add another colour to complete the shape. You do not need any additional guidelines or templates to do this – cut freely and confidently and, if you don't like the resulting shape, use the discarded piece of the paper template to recut it.

When choosing your colours, add interest to your picture by using different shades of green for the grass and trees, and different pinks and reds for the poppies. I used five colours of poppy in my picture, varying from purple buds to pink and red.

ORDER OF WORK

As before, first identify the parts of the picture in front of other things. The poppies, bird houses and bird, sunflowers, trees/hedges and the sun will need to be coloured first, but not in any particular order. I started with the poppies simply because I was excited to see how they would look – not the most scientific method!

Y●U WILL NEED

Papers: one A4 (US Letter) sheet of copy paper; one A4 (US Letter) sheet of 160gsm white paper or card; one A4 (US Letter) sheet of 160–220gsm card; selection of 160gsm paper or card in different colours

Knife: cutting knife and spare blades of choice

Glue: glue pen, glue stick and PVA glue with spreader

Other: metal ruler

The template for this project, provided at actual size.

Focus on... Colouring groups of small shapes

POPPIES

Sometimes you can create a bold effect, and save time, by colouring small, well-defined objects as groups instead of individually, providing the objects are on a contrasting background. This doesn't work so well with trees in a field for example, because of all the green. But in this picture, the strong shape and colours of the poppies will contrast well against the green background.

Build up the flowers semi-randomly, using different colours here and there and avoiding clumping the same colour in a particular area. Planning your colour palette ahead of time will help to guide you – it's easier to work out how to arrange things for a natural effect if you know exactly which colours you can use.

1 First fill the centre of each poppy. I'm using black paper, rather than card, for the centres of these poppies. This is useful if you don't want to create depth, but to have a nice flat finish.

2 In addition to individual flowers, look for pairs or small groups of flowers touching each other. Instead of cutting them out individually, cut round the outside edge of the group and take out any areas of space, such as little gaps between the petals or flowers. For a varied effect, use a mix of colours across the area.

3 On the reverse of the papercut, use a glue pen to dab spots of glue around the outside edge of all the flowers in the group, adding extra glue to the centre pieces you fixed earlier to give more stability, then place the infill.

4 As you work over the area, stand back occasionally to check that the effect is building up as you wish. Try to avoid over-thinking things; you're aiming for a semi-random effect that is pleasing to the eye – sometimes it's best just to go with your instincts.

SUNFLOWERS

You can use the same process for the sunflower petals. Fill the middle of the flower first, then, instead of cutting round each petal individually, just cut round the outside edge so you have a rosette shaped piece of coloured paper which you can stick straight over the back. I used a single colour for each of my sunflowers, but if you wanted different shades of petals within each flower, choose groups of four or five petals and cut round their outside edge instead.

For the sunflowers, although you need to cut out the individual petal shapes around the edges, the infill can all be one. Note that the centre is added beforehand.

The finished project

Lots of the coloured infills overlap the white outlines in this summery picture, adding dimension and bringing the gardens alive.

Sunflowers

Oversized rosettes of colour give the sunflowers a breezy feel.

Foreground poppies

Using various shades of red and pink helps give the poppy bed a sense of depth.

Focal figures

The simple silhouette of the couple in the centre gives the picture a story and focal point.

Caravan Friends

I love the seaside and it influences many of my papercuts. Memories of holidays by the sea as a child and then with my own children inspired this happy, nostalgic scene of retro caravans and characterful beach huts overlooked by a nearby lighthouse and bright blue seas.

PROJECT HINTS AND TIPS

In this design you will have the chance to practise cutting shapes out of the coloured infill to create an extra dimension of colour; and to use a quick way to create two-colour stripes. We're also going to change the rules about colouring an object in the front first.

ORDER OF WORK

74

There are lots of pieces to colourfill first. Beach huts, lighthouse, sailing boat, the bunting, door decorations, curtains and blinds on the caravans (follow the steps on page 76 for the blind on the mustard caravan). Then fill the grassy layers beneath the caravans.

Here's where we could take a different approach to the order of the infills. The sea is technically in front of the hills in the distance so you might be inclined to fill this space first. However, colouring the land in the distance first will make it easier to colour the sea – especially if you decide to use some freehand cutting to vary the colour of the waves. Once glued, the colourfills of the land will provide a sticking platform for the sea infills.

YOU WILL NEED

Papers: one A4 (US Letter) sheet of copy paper; one A4 (US Letter) sheet of 160gsm white paper or card; one A4 (US Letter) sheet of 160–220gsm card; selection of 160gsm paper or card in different colours

Knife: cutting knife and spare blades of choice

Glue: glue pen, glue stick and PVA glue with spreader

Other: metal ruler

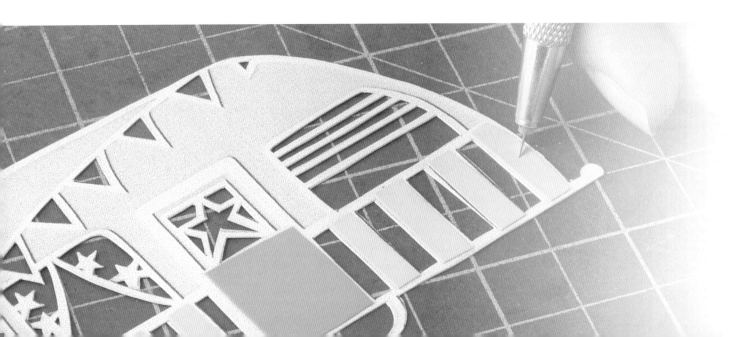

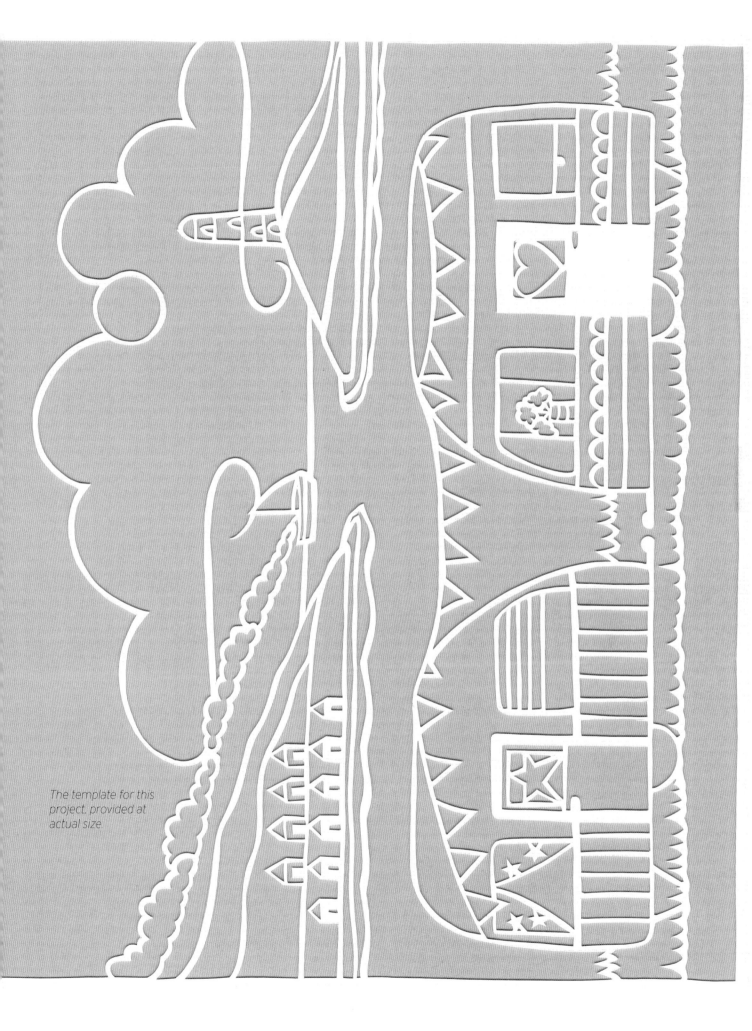

The template for this project, provided at actual size.

Focus on... Two-colour stripes

The mustard caravan has two colours of stripe: orange and yellow. Here is a quick and easy method of creating coloured stripes which will save you cutting each one out individually.

1 Take your first colour and cut out and stick the individual stripes in place. Note that the door has also been added before the large panel of the second stripe colour.

2 Cut one large panel from the second colour, and glue it across the whole space: the infilled stripes as well as the remaining spaces.

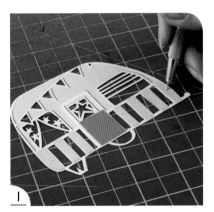

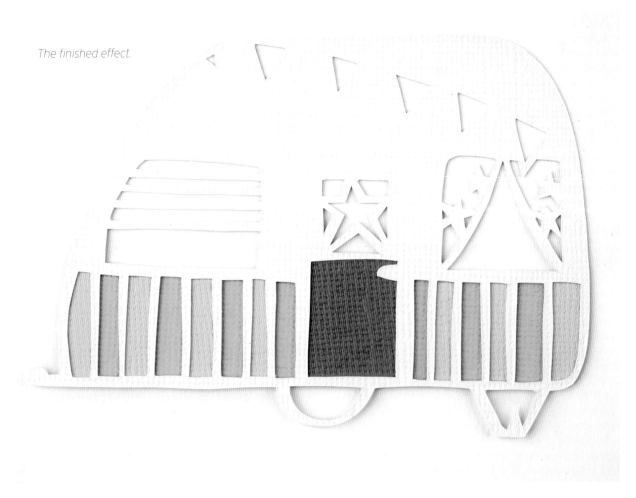

The finished effect.

Adding colour to infills

In the finished image, you will see that the mustard caravan has spots which were cut out of the top layer, with a lighter colour adhered to the back. There are three methods to do this detailed below. Whichever method you use, once your first colourfills are in place, you can apply freehand infills behind the shapes .

Note that it doesn't matter too much what the back of the picture looks like because you will stick a fresh piece of card across the back of the entire picture when it is finished to give it even more stability.

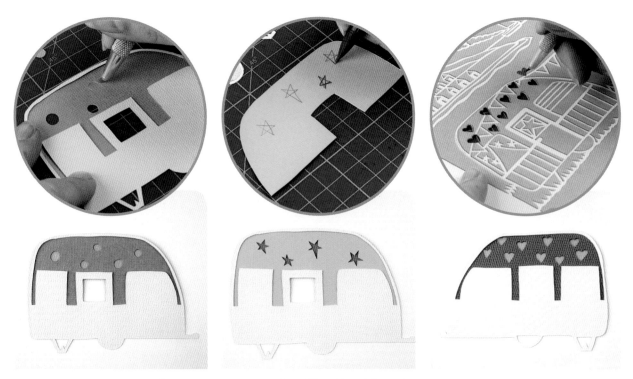

A Adhere your infill to the silhouette papercut, then cut shapes out from the right side, freehand. This has some risks – you could make a mistake and then have to remove the glued infill to try again.

B Cut out the infill and hand draw the shapes on the back of the piece, then cut them out from the back of the infill before you stick it down.

C Draw the shapes onto the template just before you cut out the infill. Cut out the shapes first, then the outline of the infill.

TIP »»»

If you are careful, you can keep the small shapes you cut out for later use elsewhere – perhaps as topfills.

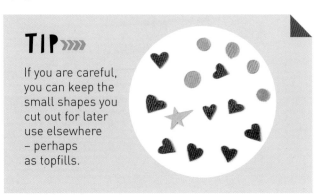

The finished project

Colours reflected from the pink caravan into the sky give this bright, happy scene a cosy feel.

Sky

Choosing your colour palette in advance means you can build a freehand sky confidently because you know all the colours complement or contrast well with each other.

Land

As well as drawing the eye into the distance, colouring the staggered landforms first provides a good sticking platform for the freehand sea colourfills.

Freehand sea

Using different shades of blue and wavy-shaped pieces gives distance to the sea and suggests different depths of moving water.

Harbour Arches

This piece is inspired by the arches that span the Royal Harbour of Ramsgate in Kent and which are now home to boutiques and cafés with views across the marina and out to the English Channel. I took lots of photographs then picked out some of the parts that I wanted to include in the papercut and hand drew them. It's not an exact view but contains enough recognizable detail to give the viewer a feeling of familiarity. I have then used my own choice of colours to create a fresh feel.

YOU WILL NEED

Papers: one A4 (US Letter) sheet of copy paper; one A4 (US Letter) sheet of 160gsm white paper or card; one A4 (US Letter) sheet of 160–220gsm card; selection of 160gsm paper or card in different colours

Knife: cutting knife and spare blades of choice

Glue: glue pen, glue stick and PVA glue with spreader

Other: metal ruler

PROJECT HINTS AND TIPS

In this template, you will see that I used 'negative space' – some of the houses and arches are left white with windows cut into them, while others have been completely cut out and infilled with colour. This is a useful design technique to use if your picture features lots of buildings or similar shapes next to each other.

Whilst the template may look complicated at first glance due to the detail and lots of colours, most of the cuts are straight lines, squares and rectangles which can then be filled in groups (see detail below).

The trickiest parts are the pathway lines that extend across the width of the picture. Cutting long, thin lines requires concentration and a sharp blade to prevent the paper stretching or even tearing and you may need to lift the knife at intervals, move the paper along, then reinsert the knife to carry on.

This detail of the back shows the simple shapes of infills that cover multiple areas. From the front, this gives a deceptively complex appearance.

ORDER OF WORK

To colour, identify the objects that are in front of other things and colour those first – the boat sails in the bottom of the picture, then the boats, gulls, windows and doors and the sun. Colour any house and arch walls and roofs, then fill the sea using freehand infills to break up the colour of the water if you wish. Add the pathways and finally the sky.

The template for this project, provided at actual size.

81

Focus on...

Colouring details not in the template

If you look closely at the arches in my completed picture, you will see that there is a dark brown outline above them which is not indicated on the template. I added this to make the arches stand out against the wall behind them.

You will see a similar effect on pages 34–35, where I added sunlit highlights to the snowy mountains.

FOR THE ARCHES:

1 Cut out the infill for the walls of the arches in one piece.

2 Turn the piece and infill over to check the fit, but do not glue it.

3 Before you stick the infill in place, use it as a template to cut a larger piece in a darker colour. You can draw round it (right sides down) if you wish, or just hold it firmly in place while you cut freehand.

4 Glue the first piece into place (see inset), then apply glue to the back of it ready to stick the second infill.

5 Place the second infill right side up on your sticking mat. Turn your papercut landscape the right way up and hover it above the darker infill until you are happy with the position, then lay it on and press firmly to stick.

6 With the second infill in place, continue with the rest of the template. Here the brick wall has been added behind.

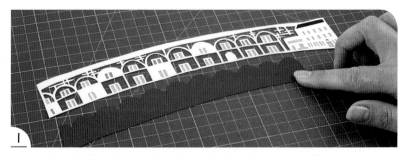

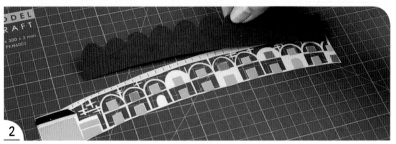

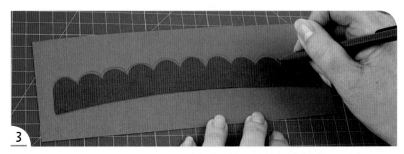

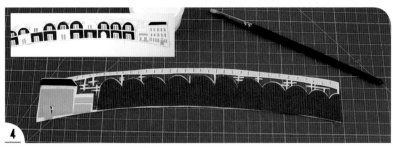

Focus on... Adding topfills

My finished picture has yellow cloud shapes in the sky, which are not indicated in the template. Adding coloured shapes to the infill is another way you can break up large spaces of colour. I do this freehand, but you could also draw your topfills onto the reverse of your coloured paper before cutting.

1 Cut out a large infill which covers the whole sky area.

2 From the right side of the card, cut out freehand shapes – clouds or swirls for example – in your second colour.

3 Place the sky infill right side up on your clean cutting mat, and position the swirls, without gluing.

4 Turn your landscape papercut right side up and lay it over the sky and swirls, adjusting the position of the topfills until you are happy.

5 Put the landscape to one side, then carefully glue the topfills onto the sky infill.

6 You can then glue the infill to the landscape.

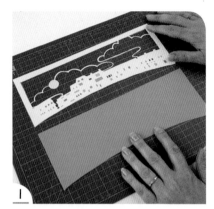

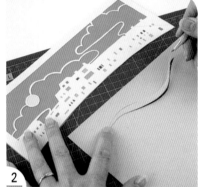

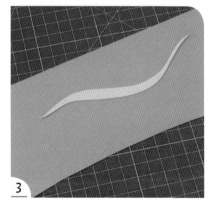

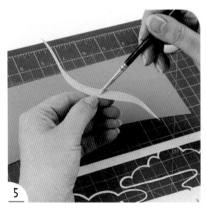

Strong colours used in the windows

Use stronger colours in small places, like these windows, so that the colour shows up against the white outlines.

Boats, sea and land

The sea is added after filling the boats with colour. This means it overlaps the harbour wall outline, which helps to create the idea that the sea is washing up against the wall.

Sky

Freehand flashes of colour, added as topfills to the deep blue sky, give energy and light.

The finished project

The bright colours and repetition of shapes create a busy atmosphere down at the harbour.

Moors Sheep

This picture was inspired by a journey to Yorkshire, a part of the UK filled with stunning valleys, woodland and dales, moors and limestone cliffs.

PROJECT HINTS AND TIPS

I used some freehand details on the cliffs to give them more shape and shadow, and also in the sky to break up the blue. I used the 'grouping' technique to colour groups of stones in the walls.

   If you decide to use the same colour schemes as me, you will need at least four shades of green to properly define the foreground and the fields behind the house.

ORDER OF WORK

I recommend doing the bottom third of the design first. Fill all the sheep and the tree trunks and the leaves on the trees, then all the stone walls and the buildings. Then, starting at the bottom of the picture, start adding your sweeping grass and muddy tracks. Once you get to the fields behind the buildings, fill the yellow field from the outside edge and across to the middle of the page, and the green field from the bottom up. Next fill all the remaining bushes and the little house in the distance, then the cliff faces and any remaining fields.

YOU WILL NEED

Papers: one A4 (US Letter) sheet of copy paper; one A4 (US Letter) sheet of 160gsm white paper or card; one A4 (US Letter) sheet of 160–220gsm card; selection of 160gsm paper or card in different colours

Knife: cutting knife and spare blades of choice

Glue: glue pen, glue stick and PVA glue with spreader

Other: metal ruler

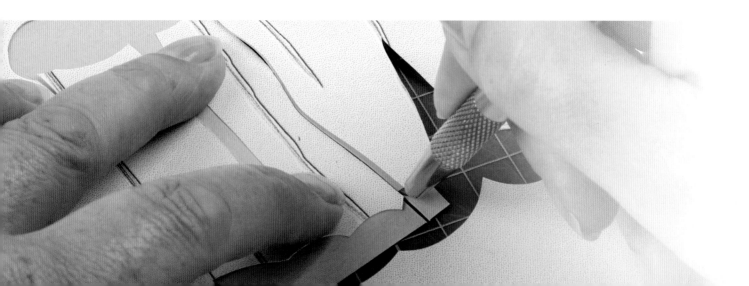

*The template for this project,
provided at actual size.*

Focus on... Adding freehand detail to textured landforms

You can use the vertical lines in cliff formations to create infills that add shadow, highlights and depth to the cliffs.

1 Start by cutting freehand pieces in a darker colour that you can stick behind parts of the vertical lines of the cliffs that appear on the template. Make these slightly larger than the vertical lines so that they create the impression of shadow. (You could also add some as topfills once the cliff face is coloured.) Next, start to cut the cliff face infills. Use the vertical lines of the template as very rough guides. Deliberately overlap them.

2 Cut slices in one colour and stick them at different places along the length of the cliff.

3 Choose a different colour, cut more slices and add those so that they slightly overlap the first pieces.

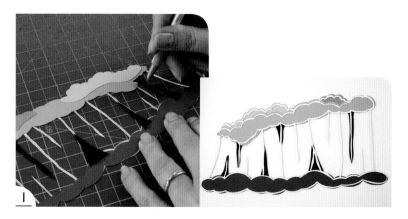

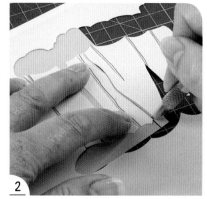

TIP »»»

If you use card, you will find that the thickness of the card will enhance the effect of the undulating edges of the cliff faces. Avoid completely straight edges, as they will look unnatural.

As well as the shadows I used four different colours for this effect, but you could alternate just two.

Focus on... Simplicity

You can make this image as complicated – or as simple – as you wish! Use fewer colours to keep it simple – use one shade of yellow across the whole field if you want, make the cliffs all one shade of cream, or all the stones in the walls the same colour. Think of the templates as colouring-in pictures – everyone will do it differently and there's no 'right way'.

UH-OH...

As your work grows in confidence and you try different approaches, you may find that your template starts to fall apart. My templates often disintegrate! If you have a photocopier handy, just photocopy the back of your papercut so far, and use that as a template to carry on, or trace another copy of the template from the book to work from.

This simplified variation of the project remains effective. It uses a smaller selection of colours – just half the number in the finished project overleaf, in fact, to give a cooler spring-like feel. I also simplified the template by removing some of the furrows and the cliff details.

The finished project

The angle of the stripes of colour in the fields follows the direction of the lines on the template. This helps to create the perspective of the farmed landscape.

Cliff faces

Use the thickness of the card to add a sense of dimension and depth to the cliff faces.

Buildings and animals

Using a darker colour for the house and path in the midground adds a sense of distance, as do the smaller sheep here.

Foreground sheep

The sheep shapes are very simple – no special drawing skills are required to create an image that is immediately recognizable. Varying the colours adds interest.

Waterfall

In this piece you will get to use your freehand skills to create infills and topfills to give movement to the tumbling waterfall.

ORDER OF WORK

Before you get to the water, you need to infill the birds, leaves on the trees, the sun and the fish, as they are all objects in front of other things. Next colour the rocks at the bottom right of the picture (they are on the left side of your reversed template), as the rocks are in front of the waterfall.

You now have a choice. Water first? Or the rocks and tall green banks first (on the left of the finished picture, or the right of your template)? If you fill the grassy banks and shrubs first, you will have a nice sticking platform for your watery infills. This is the easier option.

If you do the water first, you can cut your infills slightly oversized by not following the exact lines on the template, giving more movement where the water spills over onto the banks. This is the trickier option because there isn't much of a sticking platform to attach your watery infills too. With that said, either approach will look fine. I chose the second option because I wanted to make the water look like it was splashing over the rocks and the banks – if you look closely at the finished piece you can see where the blue has come outside the lines of the silhouette cut.

Once you have decided, look closely at the waterfall in the finished picture. It has two channels, one in front and one behind the rocks running down the middle. Working from the objects in the front, colour the widest channel of water first, then the rocks in the middle of the waterfall, and then the channel that runs behind the rocks.

Once the waterfall is in place, you can continue with the rocks and grassy banks. I kept the final part, the sky, very simple, with no freehand infills or topfills, because I didn't want to detract from the running water. You will also want to reserve a different shade of blue for the sky, so that there is a clear division with the waterfall.

YOU WILL NEED

Papers: one A4 (US Letter) sheet of copy paper; one A4 (US Letter) sheet of 160gsm white paper or card; one A4 (US Letter) sheet of 160–220gsm card; selection of 160gsm paper or card in different colours

Knife: cutting knife and spare blades of choice

Glue: glue pen, glue stick and PVA glue with spreader

Other: metal ruler

Focus on... Running water

I love cutting infills for running water because you can use freehand cutting and really play with your shapes. Providing your shapes represent the direction the water is travelling, you can't really go wrong! I used four shades of blue, but two or three shades will also work, especially if your lighter shades are positioned along the 'frothy' template lines.

1 For this simplified version, you will see I have adapted the template (see page 59 for the technique) by removing the fish and simplifying the trees. I have also highlighted the entire front channel of the waterfall as one piece.

2 When you come to the waterfall, cut out the big piece, but don't stick it in place just yet.

3 Following the direction of the flowing water, freehand cut some long, slim wavy shapes out of the big infill. Your big infill will now have shapes ready to fill.

4 Apply a darker colour to the reverse of your big infill to fill the wavy shapes you just cut from it.

5 If you are feeling particularly adventurous, you could also cut shapes out of those new infills, from the right side, and fill them again with a different shade.

6 Now use a lighter shade and cut out several freehand, wavy shapes that will be topfills. You don't need to follow the template to do this, just create shapes that roughly follow the curves in the waterfall. Have a play – lay them on top of the big infill and move them around until you are happy.

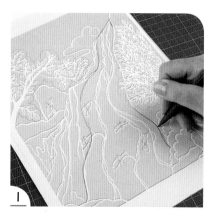

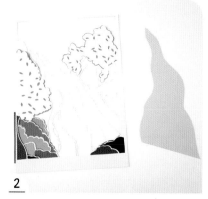

7 At this point you can try adding topfills to your topfills!

8 Before sticking, lay your silhouette papercut right side up over the waterfall collage you have created. How does it look? Do you need to add more freehand details?

9 When you're happy with your waterfall section, glue it all down, then fix it to the reverse of your silhouette papercut.

10 You can now carry on - attach the rock between the water channels before starting the second channel.

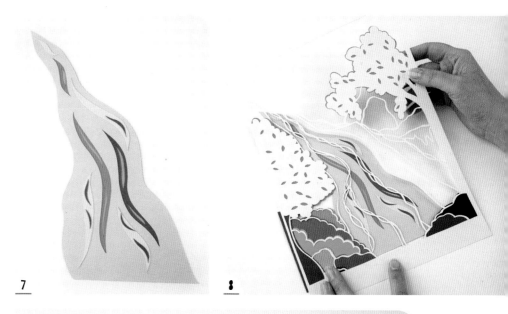

7

8

9

10

95

The finished project

Autumnal leaves add colour to the picture, while keeping the sky simple allows the blues of the waterfall to take centre stage. Dark, freehand topfills on the rocks in the waterfall add shadows.

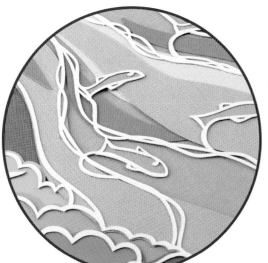

Fish

The fish in the design are connected to the template's moving water and add energy to the picture. You could use glittered or metallic paper to make them more of a feature, or amend the template and remove them altogether.

Foliage

Infill the leaves in groups and use bright colours to add vitality to the picture. For a more peaceful effect, use shades of green, reserving one shade of green to be used as the background colour behind the leaves.

97

Birds

Apart from being decorative, the birds also add a sense of distance. They are simple, recognizable shapes requiring little detail.

Early Morning Milk

When I was little, my bedroom was at the front of the house and I remember hearing the whirring of the electric milk float approaching. I could lie in bed picturing which house the milkman was going to, by the sounds of the front gates opening and closing and the clinking of the milk bottles!

PROJECT HINTS AND TIPS

Topfills showing light and shadow make a real difference to this picture. Cut them freehand, using scraps of light and dark coloured paper/card, then lay them in place until you are confident and happy to glue them down.

ORDER OF WORK

Unusually, I started the coloured infills for this picture from the bottom of the image and worked my way up, making sure to fill the shapes in front of other objects as I went. Building the picture like this can give you more of a sense of progress because you are adding large areas of colour sooner. Just be sure to check there are no objects that need colouring before you add background colours – for example, tree trunks in front of grass.

YOU WILL NEED

Papers: one A4 (US Letter) sheet of copy paper; one A4 (US Letter) sheet of 160gsm white paper or card; one A4 (US Letter) sheet of 160–220gsm card; selection of 160gsm paper or card in different colours

Knife: cutting knife and spare blades of choice

Glue: glue pen, glue stick and PVA glue with spreader

Other: metal ruler

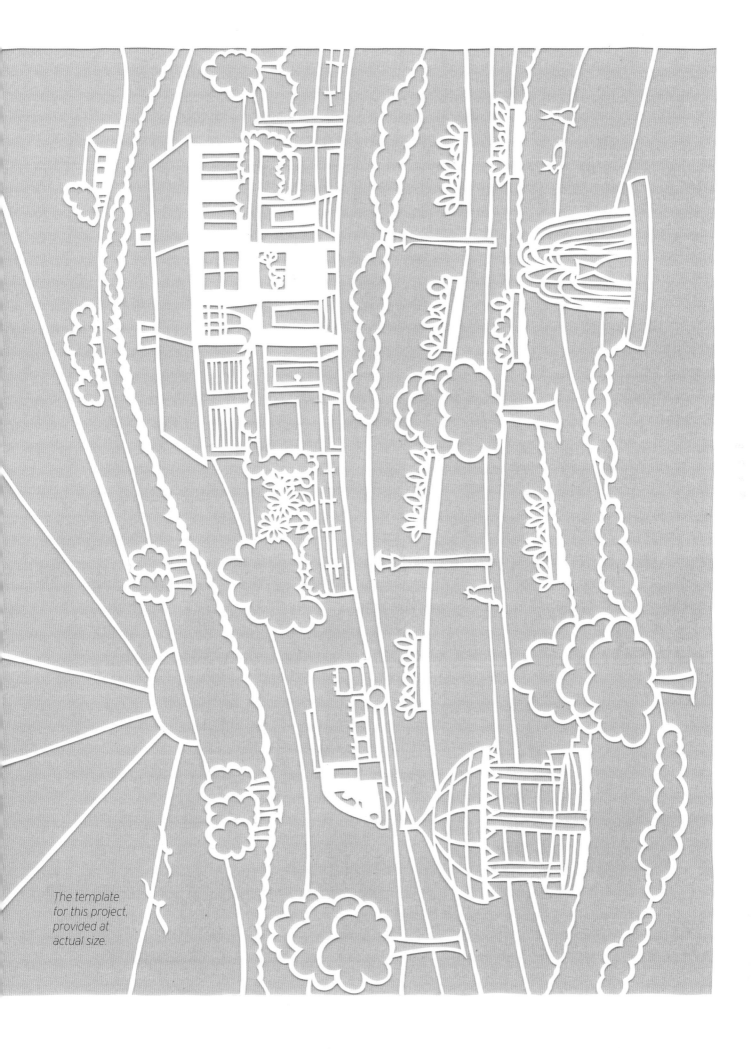

The template
for this project,
provided at
actual size.

Focus on... Working beyond the outline

Working beyond the outlines of the template is a great way to show movement and to break up large spaces of colour. Play with the paper; see how it looks before you stick it down and recut pieces you're not happy with. Water features are a great way to practise this.

1 Cut oversized infills for the fountain from a variety of blue cards or papers. You only need the basic shapes of the water in the fountain, so there's no need to follow the lines exactly.

2 The effect builds up from the centre. Having the coloured infills overlapping away from the template outlines helps create complexity and dimensionality, making it look very effective with relatively few pieces.

3 You can work beyond the outline – when adding infills in this way, add the glue, but turn the piece over to see the positioning from the front before sticking.

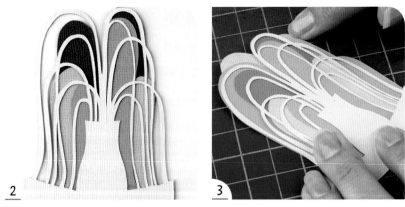

The finished effect.

Focus on...
Topfill highlights and shadows

Use your freehand skills to create highlights and shadows to further enhance your picture.

1 Cut small crescent shapes from the right side of a light coloured paper - for this early morning light, I'm using a light yellow. Keep the piece close by so you can estimate the shape and size of topfills you need.

2 The highlight will always face the source of light, so when working out where to put the highlights, imagine a line that comes from the sun and place it facing towards the sun.

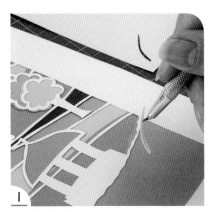

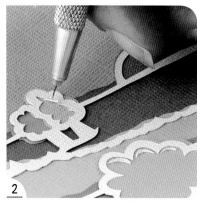

This shows all the highlights in place. Note that all the fine highlights point to the sun (the light source).

Similarly, shadows should be placed behind objects; on the side away from the sun. I used a deeper green for the shadows on these grassy hills, cutting them freehand.

Fountain

The fountain provides some movement in an otherwise sleepy picture. You could even use glittery paper for added sparkle!

Milk float

A yellow topfill highlights the sunshine reflecting off the roof of the milk float.

Buildings

If they were all in white, it would be hard to see three separate buildings, so negative space is used to break them up.

The finished project

Warm yellows in the sky and the use of sandy greens in the grass give the feeling that it has been a long hot summer in this village – I hope the residents take in their milk quickly! The darker topfills not only serve as shadows but also break up some of the larger spaces.

FINDING YOUR VOICE

I decided early on in my papercutting journey that I wanted to challenge myself by designing and making my own papercut landscapes because I love the whole process – pencil sketching, choosing the colours and losing myself in the creation of a piece of art. Since I love the seaside, this was my starting point and it is still my favourite subject today.

At first I was very self-critical of my drawing skills but I learned not to compare myself to other artists and to work with what I've got. Once you move away from what your own perception of what a 'good' artist is, you will find your natural talents shine through.

I also find that making all the tiny decisions – from choosing a subject to framing the finished piece – is a really powerful part of the creative process. You have complete ownership of your work and once you have found 'your style', inspiration gets easier and comes more quickly.

To find your own voice, be prepared to take time to experiment, make mistakes and find solutions. Focus on subjects or processes that interest you, rather than what you think is fashionable. Don't rush – you have all the time you need to get the result that you're after.

If you're thinking of designing your own papercut pictures – and I thoroughly recommend you do give it a go – here are some ways that could help.

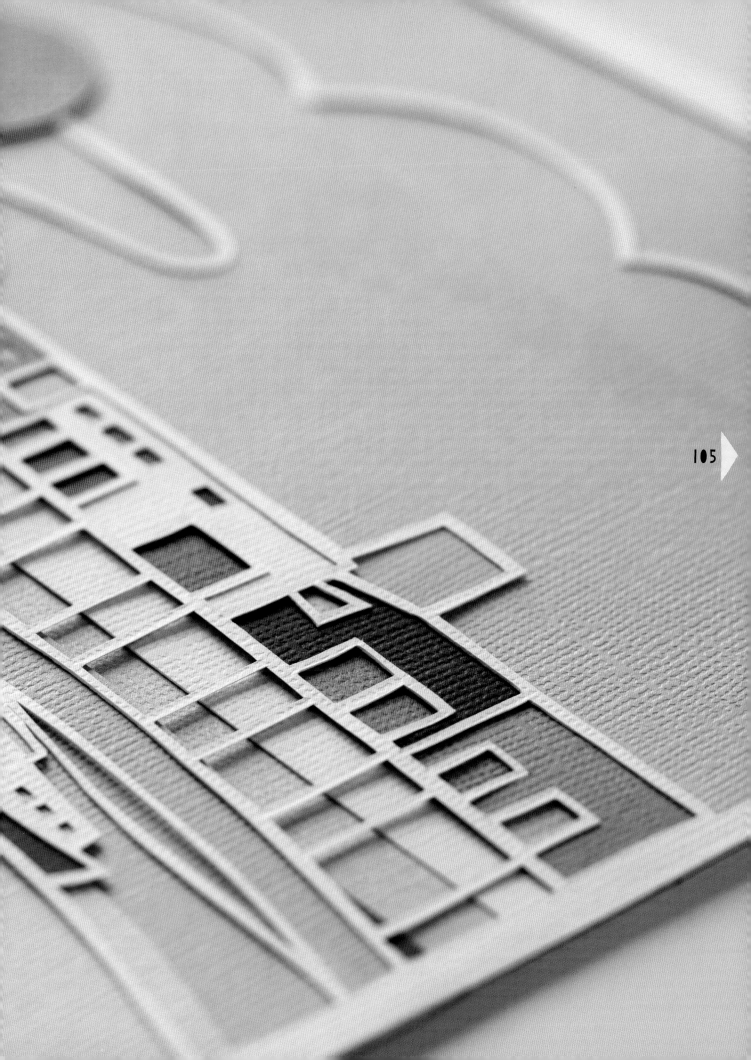

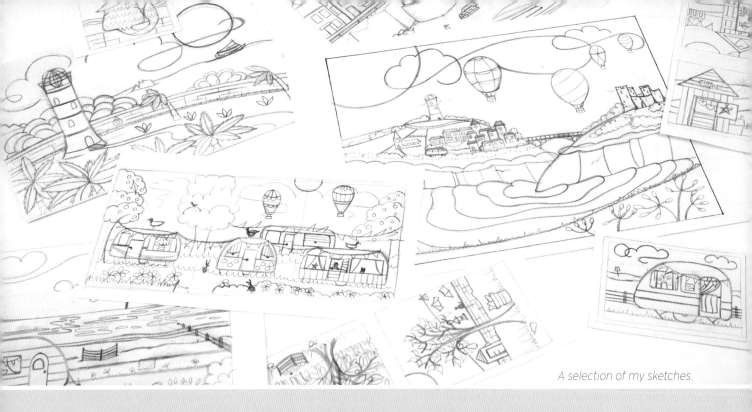

A selection of my sketches.

SKETCHING & SIMPLIFYING

To create landscapes of real places, why not spend some time with a little sketchbook in some of your favourite settings? Soak up the atmosphere while you're there and don't worry if you're nervous about your drawing abilities, because your drawings will look completely different once cut from paper. Often the simplest drawings make the most effective papercuts, especially if you use colour to add detail; in the sky for example.

Whether you are sketching *in situ* or working from a reference photograph, you're not necessarily looking to reproduce every single detail of the view in front of you – just pick out the main features and your viewer will recognize the location.

For example, in the harbour view opposite, of Mevagissey in Cornwall, I referred to my own holiday photograph, sketched the parts that I wanted to keep and left out much of the smaller detail, replacing some of the houses with green trees and losing some of the boats. The colours are also completely different because I wanted to recreate the 'essence' of the day we spent there as a family: fun, sunny and relaxing!

SKETCHING FOR TEMPLATES

In addition to simply sketching, you can sketch specifically to create a template. I find mechanical pencils best for sketching because they give a clean, consistent line and do not need sharpening. They usually have a conveniently placed eraser on the other end, too.

1

2

3

1 The first thing to do is to create a frame. Use an HB pencil and ruler to draw a frame on your paper. 15 x 10cm (6 x 4in) is a good size for a greetings card.

2 When sketching for a template, do not use any tonal work: you just need clean, simple lines. Start by drawing the main shapes; in this case, a caravan with two windows and a door.

3 Develop the other shapes, trying not to overcomplicate things.

4 In order to make the image work as a template, all the shapes need to connect to the border, either directly or via other elements. You can, of course, just use straight lines coming from the border, but with a bit of imagination, you can attach objects in more creative ways. Here I'm using a strip of grass to connect the wheel and legs of the caravan to the borders.

4

5

6

7

5 You can now add other objects. Again, make sure they connect to the border either directly or indirectly. The posts here connect to the border via the grass, and the row of bunting connects to the border via both the posts and the caravan itself.

6 Use an eraser to rub out any excess lines. This makes the template simpler and helps to avoid making needless cuts later on.

7 Don't neglect the background - some simple clouds or bushes here add interest to the background and also help to strengthen the template by overlapping other objects.

8 Once you've finished, spend a little time checking all the parts of the picture connect to the border in some way, then thicken all of the lines. This makes the lines clearer and also makes them easier to cut out later.

8

A finished silhouette cut based on the design above.

TIP »»

If you do need a stand-alone object (i.e. one that isn't connected to anything else), then draw it on as usual, and mark the surrounding area clearly – I've used an 'X' in pen – to indicate that this area needs to be cut around. You could also shade in the area you want to keep, to remind you not to cut it out. In this example, I will cut round the outside of the door, leaving the door in place on the template. I can then cut out the standalone heart shape separately. The final piece will then have a white door with an infilled heart.

To create a papercut of a specific location, a photograph is a useful reference tool. I only use my own photographs because using photographs from the internet or elsewhere requires you to seek permission from the copyright holder (usually the photographer). Using your own holiday snaps also gives you a warm and fuzzy feeling which adds to the enjoyment of making the picture!

Consider whether the view you have chosen would look good as a papercut – this might sound obvious but photographs with a beautiful, large expanse of open sky and sea, for example, can look flat and lifeless as a papercut unless you make good use of colour or add elements, such as boats or a building, for interest.

Because I enjoy the drawing challenge, I usually sketch my templates using a photo as a reference. This means I can move things around if I want to, incorporate several elements from different photographs and draw in my own style. If sketching isn't for you and you have a tablet and stylus pencil, there is software you can use to draw over the top of the photograph, or the following method will give you a realistic representation of your chosen photograph.

Whatever method you use, remember to flip the finished sketch so that the template is in reverse on your nice cutting paper, using a photocopier, computer or tracing paper.

1 Choose your photograph. The highlighted section is the part I want to use.

2 Enlarge and mirror the image – most photocopiers will allow you to do this; or you can use a scanner or graphical editing software. I also find that taking out as much of the colour from the photo as possible, using computer software or photocopying in black and white, helps to highlight the main features of the photograph.

TIP »»»

If you cannot mirror the image using a photocopier or computer, then you can simply trace the finished design following the instructions on pages 24–25.

3 Depending on the amount of the image you want to use, you may want to enlarge it further. I'm using just one side of the original picture, so I have made it bigger. Use a ruler and fineliner pen to draw the frame. I'm creating a 20 x 25.5cm (8 x 10in) frame for this design.

1

2

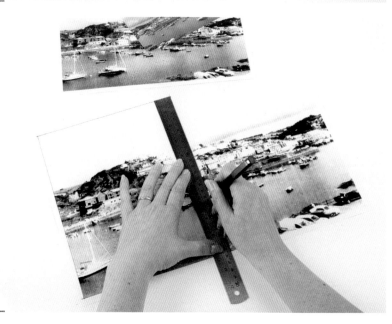

3

4 Look for the objects that stand out the most, or the ones you want to highlight, and draw round them using a pencil. Keep the shapes simple – you don't need to copy the details on buildings; just capture the basic shape.

5 Go over the lines with a pen. As when sketching for templates, make sure that all the objects connect to the border either directly or indirectly. Here I have added some wavy lines on the water, which both look decorative and serve to connect the boats.

6 If possible, photocopy the image onto your good paper so that you can use the design itself as the template. If this is impossible, then use tracedown paper or tracing paper to transfer the design onto good paper (see pages 24-25), ready to use as the template to make your papercut piece.

A finished papercut template made from the photograph.

A finished papercut made from the source photograph.

STYLE

As you progress, try to find a way to represent elements of your picture in your own style by thinking about the design, the way you apply the colour, and the colour you use. By doing so, you will begin to develop a style that is recognizably your own.

For example, people who are familiar with my work recognize how I form my clouds with a single, swirly line. Have a play with the elements that crop up frequently in your pictures – what could you do to make the trees your own? How could your buildings differ from everyone else's?

Look at how you apply colour. I often cut and stick the colourfills so that they are offset, overlapping the outlines both to give movement, and because I love linocuts and the way the print doesn't always line up exactly. What could you do with your colour? Is there an effect you could try to replicate with paper?

You have also probably noticed that my colour palettes are very similar in most of my designs because I want my work to feel uplifting and joyful. Which colours inspire you? Do you prefer muted tones, pastels or even monochrome?

Papercutting can be very time-consuming, so I recommend you design to please yourself first. Make sure your subject is something that warms you or that you are passionate about. After all, you're going to spend many hours cutting out your creation, so you want it to be something that you're enthusiastic about.

Balloons

Clouds

Coastal scenes

COPYRIGHT

I must mention copyright as many beginners are not aware of how this could affect their design.

Copyright laws exist to protect creators from having their ideas copied and sold or used to promote another business, without permission.

Photographs, song lyrics, quotes or characters from films or books, business or sports club logos, artwork, fabric and even some buildings are a few examples of things that are copyright protected.

You have to get permission from the copyright holder in the form of a license, if you wish to include their ideas in your creations. Tracing the copyright holder can be time-consuming – there are often fees payable and they can say 'no' if your work does not fit their style/image. On the other hand, obtaining a license can give your work credibility and elevate sales, if that's what you are aiming for.

Copyright rules vary according to which country you live in, so it would be wise to do your own research. Generally, there are two kinds of licenses that can be granted – a personal license which means you can recreate the idea for yourself but you must not sell it, or a commercial license which grants you permission to copy/use the idea and sell your work according to specific criteria set by the copyright holder.

Of course, you can completely avoid copyright issues by designing your papercuts yourself using only your own ideas. This approach encourages you to develop your own, unique, recognizable and inimitable style.

USING DIFFERENT MATERIALS

One way to develop your style is to vary the materials that you use. There is a huge range of patterned papers available that you can use for your infills, and you could also design your own background papers on a computer, photograph textures then print them onto paper, paint watercolour paper, or colour the backgrounds with pencils. Fabric, ribbons and patterned tapes can also be used, as can photographs, postage stamps, gold leaf and rivets... time to go through your craft drawers!

OTHER PAPERS

Pearlescent papers These have a shimmery surface and come in a range of colours from pastels to jewel-brights. Pearlescent papers can be double-sided or one-sided and usually weigh around 90gsm; similar to everyday copy paper.

Magazine pages Pick out specific blocks of text, words or letters to add to your finished design or create a collage from the images.

Newsprint You can use these just like magazine pages, but be careful not to transfer ink onto your hands and your artwork.

Glitter paper Add sparkly topfills to landscapes or use to fill shapes.

Handmade papers Often containing petals/leaves and/or thick fibres and threads, handmade papers make beautiful background papers.

Card This can be found in a variety of colours and textures. Card over 300gsm is hard to cut in detail with a knife so test-cut it first.

Original book pages, maps and sheet music These are all popular background papers. Usually you can only use the originals (as copyright prevents you making photocopies).

Balloon Trio

A printed rainbow-coloured paper covers the background. The balloons themselves are filled with tissue paper, glittered card and shapes cut from a pearlescent paper swatch leaflet – don't be afraid to look beyond the obvious for ideas!

EMBELLISHING YOUR WORK

There are many ways that you can embellish your papercut art to make it even more unique. Using glittered paper for your infills is perfect for celebration papercuts, for example. Some glittered sheets are bumpy and the backing paper poor quality for papercutting, so I prefer to buy this in person. Give it a good rub to check the glitter stays on and the backing paper is smooth.

I also like using glitter film – a clear, lightweight film covered in smooth glitter which will not rub off and is very easily cut with your knife or scissors. You can buy this in sheets or rolls.

Some papercutters like to add painted or pencil-coloured details to their infills. If you intend to paint your paper infills, test paint a piece of your paper first to see how the paper reacts as some paper may curl and wrinkle.

Try glitter pen or metallic pens to colour the edges of your infills, or to add a layer of glitter or gold to paper before you cut infills from it. The liquid in specialist pens can spread on certain papers, so colour/glitter the paper before you cut out the infill rather than after it is adhered to the cut.

You could also have fun attaching lightweight embellishments to your papercuts – seed beads, small shells and buttons, for example. Use strong glue or, alternatively, stitch them to the paper.

A selection of embellishments and embellishing tools: metallic pens, adhesive jewels, sequins, seed beads, and buttons.

Glittery Beach Huts

*Sequins, crystals and seed beads add sparkle to this
glittery seaside scene.*

Yellow Rose *and* Pink Rose

These flower-themed pieces, by British papercutter Emma King, show delicate embellishments stitched in place on hand-painted colourfills.

Opposite:
Pixie Home

Pieces of retro fabric have been added between the toadstools of this artwork, also by Emma King.

Bumblebee

*Emma King has used handmade paper
for the wings of the bee in this piece.*

Enjoy the Ride

Lisa Daniels enjoys creating handmade, three-dimensional elements from clay and experiments with fibres to embellish her papercutting work. You can also see here an example of a cut that has been mounted in two layers, one at the front of the frame and one at the back, to give depth.

DISPLAYING YOUR WORK

After spending many hours completing your papercut landscape, you will want to put it on display in your home, or perhaps give it as a gift. You may even want to sell your own designs. Whatever your intention, mounting and framing your work well will help show it off to best effect.

When I started papercutting I framed my art myself – I used supermarket frames and standard mounts if I had one suitable – but it's not a process I enjoy. There's nothing more frustrating than holding up your carefully mounted and framed picture and finding a speck of dust under the glass; so I now take all my art to be professionally framed as it actually saves me time and therefore money (and my sanity). Here is some basic information to get you started so that you can make up your own mind about framing.

MOUNTS

As well as looking pleasing to the eye, a mount will provide a barrier between your artwork and the glass in the frame. It can also give a straight, clean edge to your papercut landscape. Mounts come in many colours – I like white because it suits my white papercut lines, allows the colours to stand out and suits most homes. But if you would like to try something different, look online or take your artwork to your local framer who will be able to show you a range of colours next to your picture and make recommendations.

Ideally, your papercut will have been made to fit a standard frame size which makes things a lot easier. If not, there are businesses who will cut the aperture to the exact size you need within a standard frame-sized mount. If your mount size doesn't fit a standard frame, you will need to have the frame specially made.

Once you have your mount, simply fix your artwork to it using acid-free tape.

FRAMES

There are hosts of affordable frames in all sorts of colours and materials in shops and online. Choose a colour and design of frame that suits the style of your work and doesn't overpower it. If you are gifting or selling your work, bear in mind the décor of people's homes and aim for colours that are easy to live with.

Once you have chosen your frame, remove the glass and give it a wash in warm, soapy water. Make sure it is completely dry before replacing it in the frame and adding your mounted artwork. You can also use framer's tape on the back of the frame to cover the gaps between the mount and the frame. This will prevent damp and bugs from getting inside and damaging the artwork.

Once mounted and framed, your papercut landscape will be ready to be proudly displayed.

INDEX

Golden Caravan

The bunting was cut from old postage stamps, the curtains are tissue paper and the bushes are handmade paper. Gold metallic paper fills the top of the caravan and sun, and it is mounted on brown kraft paper.

128